the boy's book of
Hiking

the boy's book of
Hiking
Allan A. Macfarlan

GALAHAD BOOKS • NEW YORK CITY

Published by Galahad Books, a division of A & W Pro-
motional Book Corporation, 95 Madison Avenue, New
York, N.Y. 10016, by arrangement with Stackpole Books,
Cameron and Kelker Streets, Harrisburg, Pa. 17105.

Library of Congress Catalog Card No. 73-81642
ISBN: 0-88365-025-8

Manufactured in the United States of America.

contents

THE BOY'S BOOK OF HIKING

a word about hiking

"BEST FOOT forward, boys! Keep going—only ten more kilometers. . . !"

These words of encouragement were spoken recently by a royal hiker, Prince Claus of the Netherlands, as he urged on a bunch of hiking boys in Holland. They were part of the group of 14,000 hikers who were competing in the fiftieth annual summer hike, 200 kilometers long, over the Dutch countryside. Rich and poor, big and small, all were hiking merrily along on the 125-mile, 4-day jaunt. Windmills turned in the breeze and tulips made bright the flower-filled fields as the many hiking clubs and lone hikers, carried away by the joy of the road, burst into rousing marching songs.

Hiking has become one of America's major sports, too. It is a fine form of outdoor adventuring as well as a means of self-discovery and achievement. It is a sport which develops stamina and self-reliance. Among other things, hiking arouses an awareness of nature and the man-made world—and a feeling of being part of it which can never be experienced from a speeding car.

Though every boy is on his own on foot, the camaraderie of hiking binds all who hike into a band of friendly adventurers, ready to share and fare alike. Hiking develops *esprit de corps,* and a pack on the back serves as an introduction all over the world.

Hiking is a way of life, a challenge, a call to fitness and fun. This book has been written to help you experience all of the thrills and fun of hiking.

May good fortune guide and be with you as you set out on the open road.

Best foot forward, boys!

CHAPTER 1

getting
the most
out of
hiking

SINCE MAN first started to brave the dangers of endless plains, dense forests, and mountain passes, walking has often been the only way to go places.

the place of hiking
in American history

The early settlers in America hiked countless miles in their great trek westward. The men walked to save the plodding oxen from carrying extra weight on the prairie schooners. In spite of this, the going was so hard that many oxen died, while the trail-hardened pioneers lived.

Our forefathers were almost tireless hikers. George Washington and Abraham Lincoln hiked mile after mile through rough country for business and pleasure. Daniel Boone, Lewis and Clark, and Johnny Appleseed traveled on foot many thousands of miles. They also managed to record the beauty of the country and memorize or map it as they covered mile after mile. They were hungry at times and met with many dangers on the trails which they pioneered, but they reached their objectives. America was largely founded on the hiking ability, determination, and courage of such men.

dog pulling an Indian travois

INDIANS AFOOT

Long before the Indians of the Plains got horses, they hiked many hundreds of miles. The red men took all of their belongings with them, packed on their backs or loaded onto travois which were pulled by the men, women, children, and dogs of the tribes.

HOW OLD-TIME HIKERS GOT THEIR SKILL

A few professional pedestrians walked distances ranging from forty to sixty miles daily, sometimes two or three times a week. During the early 1900's, some made trans-continental hikes. The fastest walkers covered one mile in 6½-6¾ minutes. Today, seasoned hikers who walk about twenty or thirty miles a day at an average speed of five miles per hour consider that they are doing very well.

Much of the hiking skill and endurance of the old-time hikers was developed through practice and compelled by necessity, since there was practically no other means of transport.

Today, when a bus or taxi strike ties up transport in a city or town, many people who do not have cars or bicycles take to the road. They are often surprised to discover their unexpected walking ability. Some even continue to walk when normal transport has been restored. In short, they become habitual hikers. That is, they walk with a purpose.

The word "hiking" is defined both as "walking with a purpose" and as "a vigorous walk, usually across country." Both descriptions serve. When hiking or hikes is mentioned throughout this book, it means covering ground, sometimes quite a lot of it, purposefully.

In many countries, and even in some rural areas of the United States, old and young people sometimes walk from two to ten miles daily, to and from work or school. Knowing this, one is amazed to hear people who are, perhaps, suffering from

an overdose of civilization and modern transport, say, "Soon people won't need legs."

where to hike

Strangely enough, in a country as vast as the United States, there has been until recently little opportunity for hikers to climb a stile and set off on even restricted cross-country rambles. There were hiking trails, but many were difficult to reach without motor or water transport to convenient starting points. Often these jumping-off places were far away.

You might protest that there is no place for you to hike. You may say that the automobile has chased hikers from the roads and that much of the countryside near where you live is private property where hikers are not welcome. You might well say that it would take a miracle to bring real hiking back again. You may be surprised and happy to discover that this miracle is happening today in many parts of the United States.

Government and civic leaders have realized that there are millions of boys and grownups who are still pioneers at heart. These leaders are now bringing cross-country paths and trails to you. Very soon, there will be safe hiking freedom, thanks to the establishment of national trails and networks of walkways within easy reach of most homes.

Soon, boys will have little roads and trails to share with the brotherhood of hikers. On these paths no squashed frogs, crabs, or little furred creatures, victims of the automobile, will cause you to turn your head away. There will be no need to jump into a ditch or up a steep embankment to avoid reckless drivers and galloping horses. You will be on a road that has been set aside for hikers only—for you!

Safe paths and trails, with points for stopping to picnic, will soon wind their way throughout America. They will provide a fine opportunity for exercise and endurance which was unavailable when cars ruled the roads. Thousands of men are working every hour of the day to accomplish this miracle for you. They are constructing brand-new trails and reconstructing and rehabilitating others to assure thousands of miles of hiking pleasure. These "Trails for America" will crisscross the United States. They will call for hikers who have hours, days, or weeks to spend on this nationwide system.

CITY AND SUBURBAN HIKING TRAILS

Ideal hiking country is being opened up. Trails will lead not only through the countryside, but also through urban centers and near metropolitan areas within easy reach of people's homes. Clever planning has made possible the urban equivalent of rural or wilderness trail experience. These city and suburban trails are being built on abandoned railway tracks and along river and canal banks, utility rights of way, old streetcar beds, and quiet city streets.

TRAILS OF SPLENDOR

Where can lone hikers and groups hike on a limited scale? A number of magnificent national scenic trails have lured hikers from many lands for many years, though some of these trails are still incomplete. The following are the really big trails:

log shelter commonly found along the Appalachian Trail

- The Appalachian Trail, extending for 2,000 miles from Mt. Katahdin, Maine, through fourteen states to Springer Mountain, Georgia. This pathway, including lean-tos and outdoor cook places, is the result of a labor of love, contributed in large part by outdoor enthusiasts.
- The Pacific Crest Trail, 2,300 scenic miles, stretching from the Washington-Canadian border along the backbone of

the Cascade and Sierra Nevada mountains to the California-Mexican border. At the time of writing, the federal and state governments are still working on this splendid hiking route.

- The Continental Divide Trail, 3,082 miles of majestic beauty, reaching from the Montana-Canadian border in Glacier National Park through many national forests and scenic areas in the states of Montana, Idaho, Wyoming, and Colorado, to Silver City, New Mexico. Work is still in progress on this trail as this book is written.
- The Lewis and Clark Trail, one of the most promising pathways for hikers being developed as this list is compiled. It will stretch 4,600 miles from St. Louis, Missouri to the mouth of the Columbia River over breath-taking passes and along rushing rivers. Imagine a trail that will wind and unwind for nearly 5,000 miles! Why not ready those hiking shoes? Remember the little Indian girl who hiked blithely along this trail with her baby on her back!
- The Potomac Heritage Trail, only a little stretch, compared with the above paths, but packing a lot of history and pastoral beauty into its 825 miles from the mouth of the

Potomac River to its sources in Pennsylvania and West Virginia. This trail includes a lovely 170-mile stretch incorporating the Chesapeake and Ohio Canal towpath. Work is still being done on the Potomac Heritage Trail as this book goes to press.

There are other exciting trails, such as the Long Trail, 250 lovely miles of it, in Vermont. It was bought and built by lovers of hiking and the unspoiled outdoors. Dedicated outdoorsmen still maintain it in some of its most beautiful stretches.

Many other trails, shorter but well worthwhile, are being planned and worked on. At least one of them probably passes close to you, and even the huge trails mentioned above may have stretches that come temptingly close to where you live. You don't have to hike 1,000 miles, once you set foot on them. Why not think again about your hiking shoes?

hiking clubs

Hiking as a hobby and for sport is growing rapidly. Schools, colleges, and boys' clubs have formed hiking clubs and groups. The growth of hiking associations is bringing hiking to the attention of the general public and various branches of the government. Such groups have done a great deal toward securing and protecting the rights of hikers. They have helped to establish right-of-way across private lands which often blocked access to beaches, stretches of open country, lakes, and mountains.

ADVANTAGES OF CLUB MEMBERSHIP

By joining a hiking club or group, a lone hiker has the benefit of having an organization behind him which can help him extend his hiking scope. He makes new friends of similar interests and becomes an active part of a group which is able to secure a better deal and better trails for hikers. To find a hiking club or group which meets his requirements, a hiker can contact a YMCA or youth hostel, museums, libraries, newspaper offices, local boys' clubs, and similar organizations. Some city museums sponsor hikes.

Aids to hikers issued by hiking clubs include booklets, trail guides, maps, and notices in newspapers, telling of hike objectives for weekends. (In fact, many hiking organizations print or mimeograph a schedule of hikes which they plan to carry out, rain or shine, over a period of three to six months or longer.) Established groups can often secure permission to hike on private property and to places of interest, when it is difficult for an individual hiker to make such arrangements.

FORMING A HIKING CLUB

After checking up on hiking clubs and groups, a lone hiker is better able to decide whether he wishes to join one or form his own, with the help of a few hiking friends. From three to six hikers can form a satisfactory club.

A club may be given a suitable name and adopt official colors. This helps establish identity and promote group spirit. A

standard sort of sport shirt, of one of the club colors, may be worn by members. That is all that is needed as a "uniform." Members may also wear slacks or shorts of a standard color, if voted.

The writer organized a small hiking group known as the *Coureurs-du-Bois,* which specialized in bushwhacking hikes through rough country, and making new trails. This outfit had no special hiking uniform, but each hiker wore camp clothes and a gaily colored sash like that of the renowned *Coureurs-du-Bois*, after whom the group was named. A shoulder flash was worn on the left sleeve for identification.

CLUB REGALIA

All good organized clubs have membership cards, at least. Some have uniforms and insignia, such as badges, flashes, stickers, pennants, and other paraphernalia. Such regalia are decorative but not really essential, though useful at times.

CLUB LOG BOOKS

Every hiking club, big or small, should have a log book in which all hikes and events connected with the club are carefully recorded. If entries are not made, it can cause confusion later, since some things are of greater importance *after* the event than they appeared to be at the time.

All hiking clubs, and lone hikers as well, should observe a hiker's code. Even small hiking groups should have the club's code clearly stated and typed on a stout card for each member. This is the sort of pledge used by clubs interested in conservation, which respect the same worthwhile things that hikers do. Observing it will benefit both the organization and its members. For an example of a typical hiker's code, see "A Code for Hikers and Campers" in Chapter 10.

Any small hiking club should join a national or state organization. These well-informed federations are glad to help a club organize and step out as a full-fledged member. They also supply all information required on hiking trails and know-how.

sources of hiking information

If you write to any of the following, they will be glad to send you free information on hiking.

TRAIL CLUBS and ASSOCIATIONS

- Adirondack Mountain Club, Gabriels, N.Y. 12939
- American Youth Hostels, Inc., 20 W. 17th St., New York, N.Y. 10011
- Appalachian Trail Conference, Washington, D.C.
- New York-New Jersey Trail Conference, GPO 2250, New York, N.Y. 10001
- Potomac Appalachian Trail Club, Washington, D.C.

NATIONAL and STATE SERVICES

- Bureau of Outdoor Recreation, Washington, D.C. 20240
- Department of conservation in the capital of each state
- National Park Service, Department of the Interior, Washington, D.C.
- U.S. Forest Service, Department of Agriculture, Washington, D.C.

CHAPTER 2

how to
hike
the easy
way

WHEN YOU decide to fish, water ski, or take part in any other sport, the first thing to do is inspect and overhaul your equipment. It is unthinkable not to take the same precautions if one is going to *really* hike.

inspecting feet and legs

The very first thing to do is take a close look at the feet and legs. A hiker is no better or stronger than his feet and legs. Good health (if it is good health) which does not include these limbs is of little use when hiking. If the feet give out because of lack of care, and the legs tire easily through lack of proper exercise, the hiker is in trouble until he can correct these conditions.

It is most important:

- to make certain that the feet are free from bumps, blisters, and corns.
- that toes are not too much bent toward each other or otherwise out of place.
- that the toenails are healthy and correctly trimmed.
- that the legs appear to be in good condition.

No one should go on even short walks until any foot or leg trouble has been corrected. It is unfortunate that the majority of people bring foot ills on themselves through wearing ill-fitting, often too-tight footwear. How to care for feet and legs and treat their minor ills is dealt with later in this chapter.

hiking techniques

To get the most out of hiking, you need to learn certain hiking techniques and practices. Then you can set out on the little roads and trails which lead to beauty spots and adventure.

Though walking comes naturally, some people walk badly and others walk very well. A walker's style in covering a distance of even twenty yards indicates the category to which he belongs. Fortunately, most or all of a would-be hiker's faults can be corrected without much difficulty. There is a right way to hike to meet different circumstances. How to do so is dealt with in the following pages.

HIKING CORRECTLY

Always point the feet straight ahead, American Indian-style, as illustrated. Nobody can be called a hiker who walks either pigeon-toed or splay-footed, since those who walk that way cannot cover much ground. Such a walk is inefficient, tiring, clumsy, unbalanced, and unhealthy, and does not propel the body forward.

To walk easily and well, in the country or on a trail, the body weight should be balanced over the feet or just barely ahead of them. The knees should be bent slightly, with the body relaxed and the heel and toe touching the ground at about the same time. One can develop a fine, ground-covering stride with this

right and wrong ways of hiking
top: the correct way to hike, American Indian-style, with the feet pointed forward. **bottom:** the inefficient, tiring way to hike, with the feet pointing inward or outward.

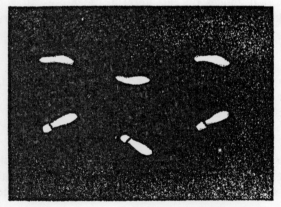

technique. The only change necessary is when going uphill or downhill, when the stride should be shortened a little to meet conditions.

Though hikers are sometimes advised to lean forward from the hips when hiking and when carrying a pack, one should be careful not to develop a "bent over" hiking posture. Such pointers should be used chiefly for hiking up steep inclines.

On pavements, smooth roads, and paths, one may stride along using the heel-and-toe technique. This should be an easy, relaxed step, with the heel striking the ground first, the toes of each foot pushing forward as the other heel touches the ground. For short distances on easy terrain, older boys in good shape can hike four miles per hour, while younger boys average three miles.

REST BREAKS

One will travel further by adopting a steady, natural pace, neither too slow nor too fast. Allow for rest breaks. After hiking two miles, stop and rest about five minutes before continuing.

BREAKING IN GRADUALLY

Even professional hikers begin with short hikes, two or three miles at the start, working up to five-mile, then ten-mile hikes. When a hiker finds that such walks are not tiring to his leg muscles and feet, and his wind becomes accustomed to even fast hiking, he advances to fifteen-mile, twenty-mile, and even longer treks. Hiking should be carried out fairly regularly. Otherwise, it is easy to lose the springy step and the fine physical condition that training brings.

PACING OFF DISTANCES

When one judges distance by the number of paces he takes between various points, he must know how much distance he covers with each step, or pace. A boy can easily tell how many feet he covers in one pace by measuring accurately, from a starting point, a few normal paces. The so-called Roman Pace is the distance between the heel of the same foot after two natural steps.

Being able to pace off distances correctly is useful for map-making and for locating things, such as a food cache or paddle, hidden so many paces from a big oak tree.

Professional hikers always establish the length of their stride and the number of paces required to cover distances ranging from fifty yards to a mile over different sorts of terrain. They time themselves by watch or stopwatch to see how long it takes to cover these distances. From these figures, they learn the length of stride best suited to the ground being covered, so they will be able to hike the maximum distance in the shortest time. Of course, professionals do not continually count the number of strides as they breeze along, because once the technique of so many paces to the mile has been established, it becomes second nature. It is often the deciding factor in winning both short-distance and long-distance races.

belt measuring tape

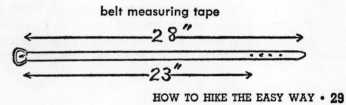

Amateur hikers can copy these practices to advantage and should learn how far they can hike in a given time, and also which length of stride helps them cover ground most speedily and with the greatest ease.

An exaggerated stride is too long to keep up comfortably. A hiker using it loses count of correct distance, once a quarter-mile or more has been paced. Also, his stride naturally shortens.

A hiker should know the exact length of his belt and the

distance between holes, so he will have a serviceable measuring tape with which to measure his paces. True, a small cloth tape measure is not bulky to take along—but try to locate it when it is most needed!

Some hike leaders and hikers wear pedometers, which measure the approximate distance covered on a hike by recording the number of paces taken. The more expensive pedometers, and even some of the cheaper ones, record this with fair accuracy.

Hiking through hilly areas has its advantages. It is good for training hikes. Even if one has to hike up a steep hill, the view from the summit is often so fine that the scramble to the top is well worthwhile. Remember that you don't have to go to the country to find hills. Many cities have hills with breath-taking views. In fact, some cities, like Pittsburgh and San Francisco, are built upon hills.

Some remarkable trails and almost invisible paths are marked in hilly and mountainous country by wise wild things which make their homes in such areas. The engineers who laid out the first routes of our western railways often found that game trails through high mountain country were better routes for the coming railroads than all their most technical surveying instruments could provide.

Deer, elk, and even domestic cattle always find the easiest way up and down steep slopes by zigzagging. Seasoned hikers and backpackers always use these trails, whenever possible, in wild country. Game trails also help in locating water holes. To anyone looking down on a plain from a height, the trails often converge on a water hole like the spokes of a wagon wheel.

All hill- and mountain-climbing should be done slowly, whenever possible. Whether climbing up or down a steep hill, the most comfortable and safest way to hike is with the feet turned sideways. This technique has several advantages, the chief being that the weight of the body rests on the entire foot. This gives more control. It is safer and less tiring than trying to go up or down steep slopes with the feet pointed forward. Also, the toes are not forced into the toes of the shoes, which can cause them to become chafed or skinned during steep descents.

Great care should be taken not to dislodge stones or rocks, even small ones, because it may cause danger to other hikers coming up or going down. This can easily happen when unseen

hikers are coming up a wooded slope. Also, rocks and stones help hold a hill up, providing fine hiking country for future hikes.

Be careful when going up or down steep places not to count on thin branches or clumps of weeds or grass to break your descent in emergencies. They are better than nothing, but grasping a tree trunk or sturdy bush, or braking with the heels and hands is a surer way to slow down the pace.

All clifflike ascents and descents should be shunned, because such slopes present problems and hazards better tackled by climbers than by hikers. It is all to the good for hikers to learn the techniques and dangers of cliff- and rock-climbing, on special occasions, under the supervision of a knowledgeable leader. However, such climbing should not be undertaken on regular hiking trips.

JOGGING

Jogging is an excellent, nearly tireless way to cover a lot of ground at an easy pace in a comparatively short time.

This efficient way to travel is nothing new to Americans. The Indians and pioneers were quick to discover its advantages.

Washington and Lincoln jogged. Today, many senators and congressmen regularly jog up and down Capitol Hill and along hiking trails in and around the nation's capital.

You may find jogging, like slow-paced running, a bit tiring at first, but it is not hard to adjust to its easygoing rhythm. Just lean slightly forward while holding your elbows against your sides. Jog on the balls of your feet, with an assist from a toe push.

Many physical training programs today include stretches of walking, jogging, running, and then walking again. Sometimes they omit the running.

Why is jogging a comparatively effortless way of making faster time when you are in a hurry? The secret lies in the role played by the leg muscles. They act as circulation boosters, carrying more than 25 per cent of the heart's load.

Surprisingly enough, although smart people everywhere have long been aware of the advantages of jogging, it has only recently caught on among the general public. Pictures of well-known people, nattily clad in jog togs, have popularized the "new" sport.

From now on, there will undoubtedly be plenty of jog parties, jogging clubs, and just plain, healthy, purposeful jogging. Soon "Jog Way" path signs will share honors with "Hike Way" signs. Special paths may even be set aside for joggers. Almost overnight, jogging has jogged from rear guard to vanguard!

foot care

All feet used for hiking require good care, even when their owners are seasoned hikers, but the ones requiring the most care are those of tenderfoot hikers. When a novice begins to hike, he should put callus pads or medicated adhesive tape over any tender spots on his feet. Massaging the feet with rubbing alcohol helps to toughen them. A good foot powder or talcum powder may be dusted inside the socks or stockings. It feels comfortable, prevents friction, and helps to keep the feet perspiration-free.

CLEANLINESS

To hike healthily, feet must be kept very clean. Hikers should welcome any opportunity to wash their feet during a rest stop. The sensation of dangling the feet in a clean, cool stream or washing them under a faucet is very pleasant. In the meantime, the socks may be turned inside out and dried in the air, preferably in the sun. Better still, a fresh pair of socks may be put on, after the feet have been thoroughly dried by towel, breeze, or sun.

Socks should be kept very clean while hiking, and should be changed as often as possible. Whenever a hiker takes off wet shoes, he should put on a fresh pair of socks after drying his feet thoroughly.

NAILCLIPPING

Some seasoned hikers like to keep their toenails cut fairly short and straight across. Others prefer to keep their nails well-trimmed but cut to follow the contour of the toes. Both methods give good results, so it is a matter of personal choice.

AFTER-HIKE CARE

The smart hiker never trudges so far in one day that he feels really tired out by the end of it. At the finish of a hike, the feet should be thoroughly examined to see that they are in good condition. If home is at the end of a hike, a hot bath upon arrival will do the feet and legs a lot of good and prevent stiffness the next day. After the feet have been washed thoroughly, any minor injuries should be taken care of. Massaging will loosen the leg and foot muscles, relieve cramp, and rest the limbs.

- Never hike even a short distance with a hole in a stock or stocking.
- Never hike wearing socks or stockings that have been darned. On almost any part of the foot or leg, the darn will rub and cause chafing.
- Never hike even a short distance with any sand, gravel, small pebble, or twig in the shoe.
- Stop immediately if any part of the foot feels as though it is becoming chafed. Cover the sore spot with a piece of fairly wide, medicated adhesive tape. If the chafed spot has already become a blister, broken or not, see Blisters in Chapter 8.
- The first thing to do when a foot hurts even slightly, in any way, is to remove the shoe and sock carefully and check on the cause. It may be a chafed spot, a seam in a poorly made shoe, or wrinkles in the sock. The condition should be corrected before putting the shoe on again.

CHAPTER 3

hikes for exploration and adventure

PRACTICALLY EVERY hike is an adventure when hikers set out for a particular destination, whether it be in a city or town or in the country. Sometimes the important thing about a trip is not the destination but the interesting things observed along the way. Hikes can be tailored to fit the special interests of camera enthusiasts or collectors of rocks, leaves, shells, or what have you. They can venture far afield or cover familiar territory. In short, they can be what you want them to be.

Remember that companionship on a hike can assure your safety. Hikes to a cave or quarry or gunkholing trips should not be undertaken by a lone hiker. Such hikes, even though they suggest fun and adventure, should be strictly avoided when you are alone, because of the risk involved. On these hikes you should go with a little hiking group, if you cannot persuade Dad, a big brother, or a grownup friend to go along. Such company can add interest and pleasure to the hike and it will certainly add to its safety.

Most of the hike ideas in this chapter can be carried out by a lone hiker. Those which cannot or should not, for various reasons, are marked *.

how tight a schedule?

It is almost impossible to estimate how long a group's all-day hike will take, unless the hikers in the group are fairly evenly matched in hiking speed and stamina. It may require a few trial excursions to find this out, but it is time well spent. Many a hiker who airily states that he has tramped all day through the mountains proves a handicap on some all-day jaunts.

When trying to figure out in advance approximately how long it will take to hike a certain distance, it is not good to estimate so many hours for so many miles. Though three miles an hour is a good average speed, the rate of progress varies with the terrain. Besides, time should be allowed to stop here and there to see interesting things. This is one of the main pleasures of hiking.

In planning longer all-day hikes for a group, at least one hiker who knows the routes should be present, to help decide on the approximate time required for the hike.

If a hiking group takes a bus to the starting point, or if part of the day's ramble is to be covered by bus, it is wise to find out in advance whether the service is good and the schedule kept. Delays and failure to keep on schedule, either on the part of the hikers or the bus company, can ruin all of the hiking plans built around the motorized part of the trip.

hiking in suburbs and cities

City and suburban hikes are often as fascinating as hiking on wooded trails. The scenery is different, of course, but the interesting things to see on city and suburban hikes are varied and endless.

When hiking in suburbia, hikers generally have a chance to

explore both town and country, using their own neighborhood as a starting point. They may cover two or more suburbs, which are linked together by good roads. Or, in some parts of the country, they may pathfind a way across country which will link two or more suburbs or towns.

This form of hiking may be varied by using one of the many transport links which usually connect suburban and urban areas, so that hikers may travel farther afield than they could if the entire outing were done afoot.

You can walk in a city or town for exercise, to visit the points of interest under the best possible conditions, or for fun. By combining these three objectives, hikers can find wonderful hiking terrain to explore.

Hiking on city pavements is tiring, so four or five miles may be long enough for the first few hikes. Most cities and towns have a lot to be discovered. In those which have colorful scenes, fascinating shops, and street scenes which amuse and divert, the miles are quickly covered. Time often appears to stand still during the hike. In some of the old towns and cities in the United States, there are curious old alleys, strange old buildings, and old-fashioned shops, tucked away in some dead-end street, where the shopkeepers sell unusual things not generally found in stores on the main thoroughfares. Too often, the exploration of old towns is limited by the imagination, rather than the surroundings.

By planning hikes in towns or cities with the help of a map and advice from a visitors' bureau, one can see much more, in less time, than by taking casual walks. A city may be explored in sections, the most interesting parts getting the most attention, and the least interesting sections, very little. In this way, hikers will have more time to devote to the worthwhile quarters.

There are a number of good ways to explore any town or city. Of course, some cities and towns are more interesting than others, but the ones nearest the hiker's home are usually the ones he will explore first. When a hiker explores a city thor-

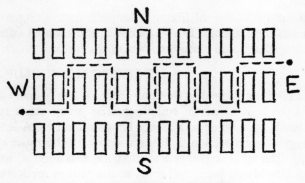

route of a checkerboard hike

oughly, he will discover many strange and interesting things, which he, and even many longtime residents, did not realize were there.

Usually, there are interesting places along a waterfront, river, or canal. In some modern cities such as New York, obstructions and "No Entry" signs on waterfront property seldom exist. One can walk almost entirely around Manhattan Island on or very close to the waterfront.

CHECKERBOARD HIKING

Checkerboard hiking is fun for one or more in towns and cities. The hikers start from a given point and follow the route, marked on a map. The group hikes along one block and up or down another, depending on the starting point. For example, the group hikes one block (or two) north, then turns left, going west for one block (or two), before heading north again, for a block or two, and then east. This pattern is repeated in the north, west, north, east, north zigzag.

A hiker or group may cover one-quarter, one-half, or all of a town or city by hiking south to north, or north to south, as desired. This checkerboard pattern may be followed from east to west or west to east just as well. Such a hiking technique avoids the possibility of hiking a long distance along a street which has little appeal. It also increases the chances of seeing interesting things and places on some of the turns.

* CHECKERBOARD JOIN-UP HIKE

This hike is arranged so that one group of two or more hikers starts from a point north, while a similar group starts from a point south, with an equal distance between the two. A leader is in charge of each section and has a map with the route clearly marked. The hike is planned so that the two groups, using a normal city hiking pace, will meet at the central rendezvous at about the same time. This central meeting place might be a small square or park.

After exchanging remarks about things of interest they have seen en route, the two groups may join forces and go in another direction, or each group may continue along the route the other has just completed.

Such checkerboard hiking gives an overall idea of the town. Besides, it may uncover fine vistas along the way.

HISTORIC INTEREST HIKES

Most large towns and cities have points of historic and/or patriotic interest. Often they contain buildings, homes of famous Americans, monuments, and battle sites, where hikers are welcome. Some of these places may even be classified as national monuments. Whether inside or outside city limits, such points of interest make good hiking objectives. They usually amply reward an hour's tour. Some such tours may even offer amateur archeologists the opportunity to discover fascinating relics without excavating, especially if they cover ground where buildings stood long ago. When these historic sites are out of hiking range from the hiker's home, arrangements can usually be made to use some form of public transport to and from the jumping-off point.

MUSEUM HIKES

In many cities, various museums have magnificent collections and exhibits of painting, sculpture, primitive art, natural history, models of great inventions, antique autos, and just about everything under the sun. Hikers' feet should be in good shape before tackling this type of tour. Covering some of these museums means a walk of several miles, and the hardwood, marble, and tile floors make those miles seem even longer.

camel

The camel is one of the many interesting animals that can be seen in zoos.

HIKES TO PARKS, ZOOS, AND BOTANICAL GARDENS

Some cities have extensive parks where real hiking may be done, as part of a visit to the city. New York, for example, has a number of worthwhile parks, such as Van Cortland, Bronx, Riverdale, Central Park, Great Kills Park in Staten Island, and Palisades Interstate Park, across the Hudson River. There is much of interest to be found in these parks, as well as space to hike. The Bronx Park has a good zoo and botanical garden; San Francisco has its fine Golden Gate Park, and most large towns have good park hiking terrain. One of the world's outstanding parks is Stanley Park, in Vancouver, Canada. It contains wild areas which have few visitors. A man used to live, rent-free, in a big hollow tree in one of its least frequented parts. Birds and beasts, wild and tame, find homes in Stanley Park, and there is usually something of interest happening within its vast domain.

Strangely enough, a number of really wild animals and birds appear to enjoy living on the outskirts of a zoological garden. They seem to be eager to join the captives inside, just as many of the zoo residents are eager to escape confinement. All wild animals, from a mouse to a blackbird, should be noted during a trip to a zoo. Points should be awarded the observant hikers who discover the greatest number of wild specimens. Very often wildlife, such as foxes, raccoons, rabbits, deer, herons, egrets, wild ducks, and geese, may be observed in metropolitan areas.

DISCOVERING THE MAGIC OF FOREIGN QUARTERS

In most large American cities, there are a number of interesting foreign quarters where the stores, streets, decorations, and dress of some of the inhabitants clearly show the influence of their homelands. The foreign nationalities vary greatly. In one city the largest foreign quarter may be French; in another, German, Italian, Spanish, Greek, Polish, Scandinavian, Chinese, or Japanese.

There is magic for the mind and eye, when hiking through foreign sections of a town or city. Strange costumes may often be seen, worn by strangers who have just arrived from other lands. Many immigrants find it difficult to part with their native headgear, aprons, blouses, or other articles of dress which they have worn for so many years.

It is an education in itself to look at the unusual articles in shop windows, such as foods, toys, and artifacts imported from the home-country. It is also fun to listen to the scraps of conversation and try to decide on the nationality of the speakers.

A group of dark-skinned men, who move with lithe grace, may be standing below the framework of a building which towers into the sky. They wear protective metal helmets. Hundreds of feet above them, a fellow-worker stands casually on the end of a narrow metal girder. What nationality are these daring men who seem to rub shoulders with the sky?

It is likely that these people are American Indians, members of the once mighty League of the Iroquois. They are as fearless in their chosen work in peace as they were on the warpath in days long past. These builders of skyscrapers are undaunted by heights. One may find them standing among the clouds atop the highest bridges, towers, and buildings in the United States.

In the Chinatown of a city, fascinating things are displayed in shop windows. They range from lovely silken gowns to jade and ivory ornaments, joss sticks, backscratchers, and scrawny chickens. The fragrances and odors are part of the scene, and if one closes his eyes, he might be in Hong Kong, Peking, or Soho.

The city hall and visitors' bureau, among other places, will be glad to give information regarding foreign quarters of their city or town. These areas have not only the characteristics of the home towns of the inhabitants, but also have movies, theaters, and various exhibitions and displays where the native language predominates.

hikes for hobbyists

There are many hikes especially rewarding for boys who have special interests or hobbies. Such hikes can be made fascinating by a leader who is fairly well informed regarding the technicalities which may crop up during the expedition. However, a *too*

magpie

well-informed leader can slow things down too much. The object of the hike should be decided in advance and may center on a particular area of interest. The following are some possibilities.

PHOTOGRAPHY

In the city, this type of hike is best when the route passes through colorful foreign quarters, shopping districts with interesting window displays, and sections containing buildings famous for their role in history or their striking design. In the suburbs and country, the trail might lead through picturesque villages or towns which provide plenty of interesting shots for the lensman hiker, or along photogenic waterways and winding footpaths where nature can be seen at its wonderful best. If such a trip is carried out by a small band of hikers, photographs of the group, taken at the most favorable points along the route, provide fine souvenirs.

MINEROLOGY

The purpose of a hike may be to discover minerals, unusual rock formations, or stones, some of which may prove worthwhile additions to a collection.

NATURE OBSERVATION

Hikes can provide wonderful opportunities to observe unusual plants, animals, and birds. Such jaunts might very well include visits to a botanical garden, greenhouse, or zoo.

These hikes are fascinating for both nature lovers and others who have not yet discovered the wonders of nature. The latter should have with them at least one hiker who has a fair knowledge of nature, as a leader.

The distance to be covered should not be long, since there will be many stops to observe plants, insects, birds, reptiles, and animals. Even a leader will not know in advance just how much time will be spent in observation. It will vary with the seasons and the number of plants and animals encountered during the course of the hike. Two or three hikers in the rear of the line should move into the lead about every fifteen minutes, so all may have an equal chance to observe. Hikers should take along pencils and notebooks, since a number of interesting things worth recording can crop up on these jaunts.

The chief purpose of all such expeditions is to develop one's powers of observation. After a few hikes of this type, boys will observe interesting things which they had not noticed before, though close to home.

Conservation becomes more necessary with each passing day and should be practiced on nature observation and all other hikes. No trees, plants, or flowers should be harmed in any way. Little wild creatures should be left to enjoy their native habitats. The few butterflies and interesting insects which have managed to escape the widespread destruction of DDT and other insecticides should be admired and not netted. Water should not be polluted in any way, and field paths should be followed whenever possible.

hikes farther afield

DISCOVERY HIKES

The purpose of these hikes is to discover little-known places within an area of about ten miles from the point of departure. The hiker or hikers may have heard of an interesting bridge, church, factory, ruin, small town, lake, stream, or wood, which will probably make a worthwhile objective. Whenever possible, the route there and back should be different. On all such hikes, enough time should be allowed to really explore and enjoy the interest and beauty of the spot.

Hikers should not be discouraged if it takes some time to locate their objective, since it is usually worth the trouble. For instance, the author organized an exciting hike for boys to find a mysterious "lost lake" in wild country at an unknown distance from the starting point. When the lake was discovered on the third all-day hike, it was found in beautiful, rugged country. The number of fish in it explained why no local fisherman had volunteered any clues.

BEACHCOMBING

Hikes of this sort provide scope and opportunity for adventure and discovery. They can be along the border of an ocean, lake, river, stream, or big pond—a lot of territory to satisfy the ambition of the most enthusiastic hiker.

Beachcombing often conjures up a vision of far-off beaches, perhaps in the South Seas, where bearded beachcombers in tattered shirts and shorts "comb" the shoreline in search of worthwhile flotsam and jetsam. Usually, not much of real value is discovered, but the excitement of the search drives the explorers on—and who knows what they may find tomorrow? Up among storm-swept islands off mainlands, and often on the mainland beaches also, valuable things are washed up from unfortunate ships which have had to jettison a part of their cargo. Occasionally, ships are sunk on jagged offshore reefs, and their sea-tossed cargos are flung onto the beach.

olive shell

Today, hikers and beachcombers may not find treasures of that sort, but other things of beauty are to be found. Lovely shells, spared by the fury of the waves, pieces of coral, polished stones of many colors, and other gifts from the sea await searchers. Often, these interesting things are to be found even when the beach has been combed by hikers only the day before, since the spendthrift sea appears always willing to renew its bounty.

Perhaps one of the finest gifts awaiting hiker-beachcombers on many shores is the stretch of gleaming, surf-fringed sand, awaiting discovery. In rocky pools, close to the edge of the gleaming sea, small fish, sea urchins, starfish, and crabs may often be found. At the high-water tideline, stranded jellyfish, shellfish, and queer denizens of the deep may be seen and studied.

A lake or a big pond in the country often has curious wild flowers and plants along its shores. Usually birds, fish, and water snakes add to the fun and interest. Rivers and streams have their own attractions, depending on their location and size.

more venturesome hikes

* GUNKHOLING

This strange word, which has not yet been included in some dictionaries, is a boatman's term for exploring a small body of water, a small cove, or a tiny bay, when the tides are right. On foot, and unencumbered by a boat, hikers can explore any

backwater of our seashores, sounds, rivers, or lakes at almost any time. Some, however, are most interesting when the tide is about halfway out. In addition to countless species of fresh-water and saltwater marine life, one may find floating and grounded cases and boxes, or even a small boat which has been abandoned because it is not seaworthy. There may be reed-covered marshes around such gunkholes in which marsh birds and shore birds live.

Many of these small bays, creeks, and ponds are often deserted, or nearly so. At such times, beachcombers and gunk-holers have these quiet waterways all to themselves. Some of these sand-bordered bays are transformed by the tides into salt marshes and mud flats, ridged by narrow channels through which swift waters run. These things add to the fun and adventure of gunkholing.

When much or all of the wading can be done in shallow water, with the sandy bottom clearly visible, this sport can be carried out without risk. If the bottom appears muddy, marshy, or too deep for comfortable wading, be sure to test it for footing and depth with a pole. One adventurous boy may hold onto one end of a stout pole or rope, held at the other end by two or three boys who are standing at the edge of the cove or bay, on solid ground, ready to pull him back.

These excursions can be carried out strictly for fun and excitement. They may also be made projects of an amateur scientific nature. For instance, the hikers can try to name the birds seen. The waterfowl may range from great blue heron to ducks of different kinds. There may also be shore birds, such as sanderling, sandpipers, and dowitchers, not forgetting the blackbirds of various species. A camera will help to record some of the things seen. A magnifying glass, or better still, a small microscope is a fine thing, too.

A dip net will bring up many small fish, shellfish, starfish, crabs, and hermit crabs from the water. A member of the group

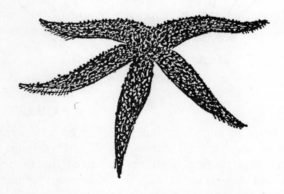

may have the good fortune to find a scallop, by feeling with inquiring toes in a sandy bottom or by dipping with a net. The creature may open its shell and peep out at the explorers. Then, they will be thrilled to see its many brilliant blue eyes shining like precious stones. When released, it will jet away.

Interesting and sometimes rare shells can often be found on the sandy beaches of inland backwaters and bays. Some of the shells will have been washed in from far-away places by storms, while others will be the common varieties which are generally found in such places.

Flowers often border little bays and backwaters. When the water is fresh, a number of small animals, and perhaps even deer, may be seen drinking at the edge of the water. Some of the pools and backwaters discovered may show no signs of having been visited before. These are fine places for shore picnics.

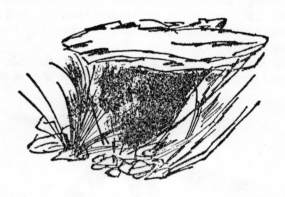

* QUARRY HIKES

For these, an interesting quarry has to be within reasonable hiking distance from the starting point, or there must be easy transport to a starting point not far from the quarry. Stout hiking shoes with non-skid soles should be worn for these hikes.

Such a hike can be completely around the quarry or to any

part of it, depending on the size of the quarry. The hikers should beware of the dangers of going too near the edge of the quarry at any point, especially when the quarry holds water, which is usually the case. They should also watch out for the danger of slippery rocks, caused by water, damp, or moss covering them. The group should take advantage of paths which often border such quarries.

Quarries are nearly always fascinating because of striking rock formations and colors. Additional interest is provided by the mosses and plants which border them. The quarry pools may be inhabited by fish, frogs, and sometimes crabs.

Even on hot days, the hikers should not swim in any quarry they visit, since the pools are often very deep, and sharp rock formations may lurk just out of sight, close to shore. Occasionally, in thoroughly explored quarries, a swimming area is marked where hot hikers may swim under supervision.

* CAVE HIKES

This is another fairly risky type of hike. The hikers should be keenly aware of the possible dangers of getting lost in the larger, tricky caves, and the chance of falling rocks. These dangers lie chiefly in unexplored caves. In them, the hikers should carry good flashlights, a few fat candles, plenty of stout, strong rope, and easily seen trail markers. The group should *never* stray from Indian-file formation. All advance exploratory work should be done by the most experienced hiker.

Hikes with unexplored caves as objectives are not recommended. On hikes which pass through or near cave country, the temptation to visit the caves is strong in hikers of any age. Nevertheless, it is wise to remember the dangers that may lurk in them.

CHAPTER 4

hikes for fun and building skills

OFTEN HIKES are taken just for the fun they provide. Certain hikes, besides being fun, improve a boy's general hiking ability by training him in special skills and increasing his stamina.

Most of the hikes discussed in this chapter are more suitable for group than for lone hiking. Some of the hikes, like follow-the-leader, cannot be taken alone. Others should not be taken alone. In this category are after-dark hikes and swim hikes (unless there is a lifeguard on duty at the swimming place). As in the preceding chapter, those hikes which cannot or should not be taken alone are marked *.

stunt hikes

At least once during the average hiking season, a stunt hike can be staged, with surprising and amusing results. A hiking group might choose one of the following hikes:

* HOBO HIKE

All members dress in character, carrying rations and gear wrapped in a bright bandanna on the end of a stick. Patched dungarees and a T-shirt or other shirt that has seen better days complete the costume. Passers-by are always intrigued and sometimes needlessly alarmed by such "hobo" groups who, though they behave well, are more or less suspect because of their garb.

* GYPSY HIKE

This is also fun. The costuming can be more or less of the

hobo type but is given added color by hikers wearing bright bandannas on their heads and flashy, big metal earrings.

* FAKE FOREIGNER HIKE

This amusing hike requires no special costume other than the usual one worn on hikes. The fun on this hike—and at times it can become hilarious—lies in the fact that the group is supposed to be French, Spanish, Italian, Greek, or some other nationality. Any questions regarding route, distances, eating places, and so on, may be asked passers-by only in the language agreed upon before the hike begins. Sign language is used only as a last resort. It is fine when one or two of the hikers speak enough of the language to enable the group to pass as the nationality they have chosen. One of the hikers should carry some sort of identification in case a policeman or someone else tries to make an issue of the masquerade.

* SECRET MISSION HIKES

This sort of adventure can only be carried out to advantage on country rambles or on trail hikes where not many people are around. This hike involves taking good cover in a hurry, stalking, alertness, and observation. Four to six hikers pretend that they are on a secret mission in enemy country and must not be spotted by *anyone*. Seeing anyone without being spotted counts high in the strategy of this hike-game. Once they have reached their objective, the hikers return to the starting point by the easiest route or any other way, decided on by the leader or by popular vote.

* SING-SONG-RHYTHM HIKES

Hikes of this sort should cover short distances, one or two miles in each direction. Hikers will find that the things they learn on this hike are very useful on long hikes, when the going is very rough, and they still have a long way to go.

During this hike, the boys sing or chant suitable tunes with a marching lilt. Each hiker may sing a suitable song and the others join in the chorus, or all members of the group may sing a popular song. If the boys decide to march in rhythm, one or more may count cadence. One of the well-known cadence lilts begins, "Left, left, I had a good home and I left." Such singing helps hikers forget that their feet hurt and they are tired.

* FOLLOW-THE-LEADER HIKES

This is a simple form of beeline hike, useful to harden the muscles of those who are not in good hiking form. It meets the needs of younger, inexperienced hikers.

A capable leader should lead this hike. The route which he takes across country is followed by all hikers in the group. He endeavors to make the hike as demanding and exciting as possible, without being too hard for younger and less hardy hikers. After preliminary training hikes, the route can be made longer and more difficult.

Younger hikers are especially fond of the mystery and adventure of this sort of hike. Under able leadership, they do not know where they are going during any part of the hike. They see ahead of them insurmountable obstacles which the leader manages to bypass, and are kept guessing.

seasonal hikes

* SWIM HIKES

Swim hikes are always popular during the summer months and, for the hardier hikers, in late spring and early fall. A vote decides which convenient lake, river, or seashore will be the objective of this hike. Ample time should be allowed for a good swim and exploration of the water edge before starting on the return trip. Hikers should take their bathing trunks and either a prepared lunch or food that can be cooked on the shore. Usually, hikers are allowed to build a small fire close to the water's edge. Outdoor fireplaces are often already installed for the convenience of hikers or day campers. Any cooking should be of the simple, quick sort described in Chapter 5.

This is the sort of hike which in some cases is best begun and ended by a short bus ride. Alternatively, hikers might hike one way if they get off to an early start and ride back. Time, distance, and weather help to decide.

WINTER HIKES

Before setting out on a winter hike, the parts of the body which are most vulnerable to cold (i.e., the stomach, feet, hands, and ears) must be protected. See Chapter 6 for what to wear on winter hikes.

Cold-weather hikes can be fun even in unsettled winter weather, when the traveler is clad to assure warmth and dryness. The contest with the elements can add interest and tough-

narrow, Cree-type snowshoe

ness to the hike and, when the objective has been reached, the hiker experiences a sense of well-being and a feeling of achievement. When he stops for lunch, he can build a windbreak with snow, when necessary. There is no risk of a fire spreading when snow surrounds it, but it should be built on bare ground or a stick platform. It would disappear, if it were built directly on top of deep snow or a snowbank. Whenever possible, a simple meal should be cooked. Hot chocolate is doubly appreciated on such invigorating outings.

Cross-country hikes on snowshoes provide much fun, some falls, and fine exercise. These expeditions can only be taken across suitable country and are enjoyable, as is skiing, only when the snow is "right," or nearly so.

The narrow, Cree type of snowshoe is by far the best for cross-country hikes. Those who own the bearpaw-type snowshoes can use them best for plodding on soft snow, rather than cross-country expeditions.

hikes for training and conditioning

COMPASS OR BEELINE HIKES

One may be all at sea in trying to find the way by compass in a big city, but it is fun. Also, it is possible to learn things about the city's streets, alleys, backyards, and buildings that would not become apparent in any other way. The idea is to travel along as straight a line as possible to the objective. This may mean asking permission to go through strange courtyards. It may even involve going in one door and leaving by one on the other side of a public building, in an endeavor to hike as the crow flies.

This hike is most fun in older city neighborhoods where the streets run in all directions, and one really has to pathfind the way. Even if the objective—which may be a skyscraper, church, or bridge—is reached only after considerable deviation from the compass line, such pathfinding provides fun, interest, and frequent surprises.

When such a hike begins in fields or woodlands, it is fun to go as straight as possible across country to some well-known landmark, visible or not, at a certain distance from the starting point. The distance must be based on the extent of the country suitable for such a ramble, and the ability of the hiker or hikers. In open country, free from "No Trespassing" or "Posted" signs, compass-direction hikes can be thrilling. They are not too easy even for older and more experienced hikers. No matter in which direction the hike goes, the route should be as direct as creeks, streams, or rivers will permit. Really rugged country, including thorn patches, minor swamps, and hills should be conquered en route. It is best to choose the easiest and most direct way home.

* CONSERVATION HIKES

These hikes can be not only interesting but also of great service to the community. When the hike lies along a river or stream, the hikers can clear obstructions from clogged waters, rescue fish trapped in shallow pools, and report pollution to the authorities. Under qualified leadership, boys may clear undergrowth from paths bordering streams, trim obstructing branches, and singe caterpillars and their tents from low-hanging tree limbs. However, permission should first be obtained to do these things. No property owner is glad when unauthorized, though well-meaning, hikers cut loose with hand axes or knives in a misplaced effort to help in much-needed conservation.

* AFTER-DARK HIKES

Hiking on busy thoroughfares after dark can be rather risky, without due precautions and adult supervision. However, such hikes are useful, since they can condition hikers to situations they will encounter when caught after dark, returning from a long hike.

These hikes can begin soon after the evening meal. The hikers decide where to meet and at what time. At least two of the hikers bring oblongs of white cloth, measuring about 12 by 18 inches. Four hikers each bring a good flashlight. Each hiker has a white armband, made from a strip of white cloth four inches wide. There may be four to ten boys in the group.

The first night hike should be along a secondary road, whenever possible. The boy in the rear wears one white oblong fastened to his jacket or shirt, while the leader wears the other one. He leads the group, hiking in single file, facing the oncoming traffic. Flashlights should be carried but used as little as possible.

This sort of hike should cover only two or three miles to the objective, with the return hike covering the same or a different route. Though any boy may be given the tail-end position, the most experienced hiker should hold the leading one. A hike of this sort is challenging and enjoyable.

After such trips have accustomed the hikers to the darkness, small groups may venture on cross-country trips, following well-defined trails for comparatively short distances. Flashlights should be carried for emergency use only and should be used only by the front and rear hiker. Just how long these hikes should be, the scope of the action, and the terrain to be traversed, should be decided by the older hikers in accordance with the average age of the group.

Hiking by moonlight is a delightful way to cover country, once one has become used to the more difficult hikes in the dark. Even across country which is quite familiar by daylight, landmarks will appear eerie, and trees and bushes will take on mysterious, sometimes spooky shapes. On nights which are lit by a near-full moon, such hikes present very few difficulties, especially when an experienced hiker goes along. They will provide much pleasure and excitement for all who take part in them.

A moonlight hike in cities or towns can be exciting. The moonlight adds beauty and mysterious effects to such hikes.

HILL HIKES

On these trips, hikers set out to climb as many hills as possible within a certain radius from the starting point. Such a hike provides fine exercise and assures interesting views of the surrounding cityscape or landscape. Flat stretches between the hills relieve the effort of climbing, and hikers should take full advantage of these easy routes.

Lunch may be eaten on top of the hill which affords the best view. If a group is taking the hike, contests may be held afterwards in which the hikers try to locate points of interest within sight of the hilltop. A boy who is good at locating such places can make this hike a fascinating one, depending on the height of the hill and the topography surrounding it. He might award points for the first hiker to point out a train, an unobtrusive bridge, a famous skyscraper, a factory, a stream or pond in the distance, a soaring bird, or an animal, domestic or wild.

Because of the encroachment of civilization, hills to be climbed in the public domain may be easier to find in or near towns and cities than in the country. A hilltop view of a city may be especially revealing and provide almost an aerial panorama with fascinating geometric patterns clearly showing how the city is laid out.

CHAPTER 5

keeping your stomach happy

NOTHING SPOILS the fun of a hike faster than an upset stomach. By assuring himself an ample supply of pure food and drink, however, a boy can easily avoid such trouble.

pure food and drink

One is so accustomed to clean, good food at home, that he is apt to forget that food picked up casually at some eating place on the road may be contaminated by unclean hands, age, houseflies, bluebottles, etc. An unwrapped, perhaps not-too-fresh meat sandwich which has been host to flies while awaiting its final consumer may bring a hiker down. A boy may eat on the road any number of times without ill effect, but only one experience with spoiled food will be enough to convince him that he should be careful about where and what he eats while hiking.

The rule on the road is to pick and choose with great care, especially if you must eat at a not-too-clean roadside stand. Food of this sort makes even simple sandwiches brought along from home seem delicious.

Be sure, also, to avoid unripe apples and other fruit. Do not eat any fruit on private property. Not only is it stealing, but the fruit may have been sprayed with poison to protect it against insects.

The right sort of meal at the right time is just as important as good meals, if the stomach is to be kept happy. For instance, a rather light but nourishing meal is best before tackling some difficult, hilly area. A boy is better equipped for such hiking without a loaded stomach, and the next full meal after reaching flat country again will seem more wonderful than usual.

For hikers, milk should be considered a food drink, and good water as a thirst-quencher. Fresh milk, however, does not keep well, even in a thermos bottle. Milk must always be used in a few hours, unless you freeze some of it into cubes and drop them into a large-mouthed thermos. Another choice is pow-

dered milk mixed on the spot at lunch. Other good food drinks are hot or cold chocolate or cocoa, chicken or beef bouillon cubes dissolved in boiling water, lemonade, limeade, or some other favorite fruit drink. All these drinks can be carried in a thermos bottle.

Never put soda pop in a thermos bottle, as it will explode. It is a bad idea to take along carbonated drinks, anyway, because hikers cannot walk well when charged with gas. Although they are tempting, ice-cold beverages should also be taboo.

SAFE DRINKING WATER

It is a good idea to take a full canteen of pure water from home or some other sure source. By using only clean water on the road, boys can avoid most stomach trouble and more serious infections. On the hike, filling stations, stores, and even private householders will fill the canteen in return for a cheery "Please" and "Thank you!"

Water from a sparkling brook, stream, or spring by the way-side is almost a sure source of dangerous infections, these days. The greatest danger lies in the fact that they *appear* to be clean. The water may flow over golden sand or white gravel and taste all right. It may be very cold—a wonderful thing to a hot, thirsty hiker. But if the water is polluted, not only stomach troubles but also serious infections may result. It is a very good rule never to count on water from such sources being safe to drink, no matter how clear and sparkling it appears to be.

If a hiker uses one of the standard water purifiers on sale in many drug and sporting goods stores, he may drink even suspect water. One of the best-known purifiers is Halazone, in tablets, but there are others equally effective. Always follow instructions carefully.

Water may also be made safe to drink by boiling it hard for ten minutes. It will taste flat, but there is a cure for that. Let the water cool; then pour it from one clean pot or jar to another several times, so the water is aerated. An easier way to improve the taste is to add a little lime or lemon juice or powder to the water, until it tastes pleasant. Incidentally, a lemon or lime tucked in your pack makes a good thirst-quencher.

how much food?

A healthy hiker with a healthy appetite requires, according to his age and size, one and a half to two pounds of food daily. The weight of the food is of minor importance, compared with its nutritive value. When a hiker uses only the dehydrated, high-value foods (meats, vegetables, and desserts) available these days, it is quite easy to keep within a daily food weight of one pound.

How well a boy eats during a hike lasting one day or more depends on how much food he takes along, what sort of food stores and eating places are to be found on the road, and whether it is possible to light cookfires somewhere en route. Money figures in such long hikes, if they involve one good meal per day in a restaurant or hotel. Such eating places, however, may not be situated on or near the hike route.

From all these considerations, it is easy to figure out that your best bet is to bring along your own food from home. But what to bring?

sandwiches with staying power

Those who have to take sandwich lunches to school or work often are not very enthusiastic when sandwiches are mentioned. This is not surprising, but perhaps a few new ideas about sandwich-making may make such meals more tempting.

The following ideas leave room for the likes and dislikes of individual hikers. There is really great scope if one takes a favorite sandwich and adds a well-thought-out plus which can make the sandwich doubly attractive. Such plusses as pickles, olives, sauces, and the like can make all the difference in meat, poultry, egg, cheese, raw vegetable, or peanut butter sandwiches. Use two sorts of bread, with slices of the same size, white and brown, for instance. Spread one of the plusses on one side and the main filling on the other.

All sandwiches should be wrapped in wax paper, foil, ready-made plastic bags, or one of the new wraps on the market. Since sandwiches form the main course of a rucksack meal, they should be nourishing as well as tempting and tasty. The number of sandwiches depends on the capacity of the hiker. When unsliced bread is used, the slices may be cut thicker to satisfy big appetites. Thin-sliced bread should not be used as a rule, but if it must be, estimate three or four slices as equal to two normal slices.

The following suggestions are for easily made sandwiches, suitable for outdoor appetites. Double- and triple-decker sandwiches are not included because, though they look pretty, they are apt to fall apart during the hike.

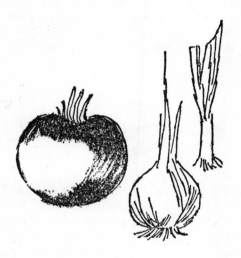

SANDWICH BREADS

Some breads which add variety to sandwiches are:

Enriched white	Rye, plain, or with sesame or caraway seeds
French	Boston brown, in cans
Italian	Date-nut, in cans
Potato	Orange date-nut, in cans
Cracked wheat	Various rolls, including special ones for hamburgers and frankfurters
Whole wheat	Raisin
Pumpernickel	

MEAT AND POULTRY SANDWICHES

Here are some ideas for meat and poultry sandwiches, along with the sorts of bread on which they taste best:

Meat	Bread	Garnish
roast beef	white or rye	pickles, horseradish sauce, mayonnaise, catsup
corned beef	white	pickles, horseradish sauce, mayonnaise, catsup
ham	white or rye	pickles, horseradish sauce, mayonnaise, mustard
lamb	white or whole wheat	pickles, horseradish sauce, mayonnaise, catsup, mint or red currant jelly
bacon	white or whole wheat	pickles, horseradish sauce, mayonnaise, catsup, peanut butter
chicken	white	pickles, horseradish sauce, mayonnaise, cranberry sauce
chopped chicken liver	whole wheat	mustard, cranberry or other sauces

thin ham-burger	rye	pickles, horseradish sauce, mayonnaise, catsup
veal	rye	pickles, horseradish sauce, mayonnaise, catsup
turkey	rye	pickles, horseradish sauce, mayonnaise, cranberry sauce
liverwurst	rye	pickles, horseradish sauce, mayonnaise, mustard
salami or pastrami	whole wheat	mustard, mayonnaise, or sauces

You can give extra tang to mayonnaise by flavoring it with curry, chili powder, or mustard. Cheeses, such as Swiss, Parmesan, Roquefort, Cheddar, American, or cream, go well with the above meats. They can be used sliced, powdered, or as spreads.

FISH SANDWICHES

Good spreads can be made from canned fish or shrimp. Mince salmon, tuna, sardines, or shrimp. Then add a little lemon juice, sweet pickle relish, chopped celery, and mayonnaise. Chopped green pepper may be added if desired.

EGG SANDWICHES

Strips of medium-hard-boiled eggs may be used as a filling, with chopped crisp bacon and chives added. Mayonnaise, thinly spread, improves most egg sandwiches. So do chopped olives, raw carrot (grated or in thin strips), diced celery, pickles, or chili sauce, according to the hiker's preference. Devilled egg filling may be made by mashing hard-boiled eggs with a little mayonnaise and relish to form a smooth paste.

CHEESE SANDWICHES

Cheeses, such as Swiss, Cheddar, American, cream cheese, or any soft spread which comes in jars, make fine fillings. Chopped sweet pickles or olives, relish, or chili sauce may be lightly spread on some of these fillings. A layer of meat, tongue, crisp bacon, or egg may be placed on them, as well. Raisins, chopped dates or figs, shredded pineapple, sliced or shredded carrots, diced celery, and other vegetables and fruits go well with most of these cheeses.

BANANA SANDWICHES

A peeled banana, sliced lengthwise and sprinkled with brown or white sugar, makes a good filling. Lettuce with cream cheese or peanut butter makes this an even more nourishing sandwich. The banana will become brownish but does not spoil on a day-long hike.

RAW VEGETABLE SANDWICHES

These can be made from various vegetables, shredded, cubed, or cut in thin strips. Some suggestions are:

Chopped water cress, sliced radishes or cucumbers, mayonnaise.

Grated carrots, raisins, chopped nuts, mayonnaise.

Chopped celery, green pepper, radish, mayonnaise.

Chili sauce or some favorite salad dressing may be used instead of mayonnaise. This varied list is set down to start sandwich-makers thinking of their own favorite combinations.

A lettuce leaf, salted and spread lightly with mayonnaise, goes well with most of the meat, fish, egg, cheese, and vegetable sandwiches above.

Sandwiches can often be fixed during a hike, if the itinerary includes a stop at a picnic grounds. Here are some possibilities:

OPEN-TOP SANDWICHES

Top one slice of favorite bread, roll, or muffin liberally with meat, poultry, egg, cheese, or some other spread. A favorite sauce, such as tomato or chili, covers the sandwich.

Sweet, dessert-type sandwiches may be made by topping a cream cheese base with fruit, such as blueberries, strawberries, raspberries, blackberries, sliced peaches, banana, pears, apples, etc.

CLUB SANDWICHES

These can be made with or without a third slice of bread sandwiched in between the top and bottom slice. The first layer of filling consists of meat, chicken, cheese, and the like, and is covered with the second slice of bread. This is topped with a slice of lettuce, grated vegetables, peanut butter, tomato, water cress, or a favorite marmalade or jam, then the third slice of bread. If the center slice of bread is omitted, use the lettuce leaf to support the second layer of ingredients.

MIDGET SANDWICHES

Miniature sandwiches can be made by using thin slices of apple, topped with cheese, raisins, or chopped nuts. The lower slice may be spread with cream cheese only.

Soups go well with sandwiches. A hot or cold creamed soup or consommé can be carried in a thermos bottle or thermos jar.

bonus bites

These tasty tidbits add zest to any lunch and often save cooking chores. Each bonus bite should be neatly wrapped in wax paper, plastic, or foil. You can use:

olives, ripe and green, mixed	pickles, mixed or not
carrots, in strips or cubes	cheese-filled celery stalks
potato chips	peanuts, *un*salted
coconut, fresh, sliced, or grated	nut meats or shelled nut mix

raisins or raisin and nut mix	nut-coated cream cheese squares
a fig bar or two	candied orange or grapefruit peel
stuffed dates or prunes	an apple, pear, banana, plums or other fruit
pineapple cubes	a small fruit tart
a cupcake	a small packet of cookies
marshmallows	coated chocolates (which do not melt easily)

or other favorites.

hot meals

If it is possible to light a small fire at some point on a hike or to use an outdoor picnic area, where there are usually fireplaces, a hiker can fix a simple hot meal. Cooking utensils are described in Chapter 9.

COOK FIRES

Check before lighting any fire, since a fire permit is often required and sometimes fires are banned altogether. Only a small fire is needed for cooking.

First collect the fuel and prepare the fire for lighting. Then prepare the food, and when it is ready to cook, start your fire. You can do so with a match and a few pieces of rolled-up newspaper, covered lightly with some dried leaves or grass and light, dry twigs. As these burn, add slightly heavier dry twigs or pieces of slim, dead branches. These may be broken into short lengths by stepping on one end and pulling on the other until the branch snaps. Branches of any sort should never be broken across the knee. When the fire is really hot, start cooking the food.

One or two lightweight miniature stoves, using canned fuel, are on the market, but most hikers manage without this extra weight.

FOIL COOKERY

A good way to avoid carrying cooking gear on a hike is to take some foil along. Hamburgers, frankfurters, etc. cook quickly and well in foil. Just wrap them well and twist the ends

food wrapped in foil

of the packet as shown, so the juices will not leak out. Vegetables may also be cooked in this way. Let the food cook in the embers or over a small, clear-burning fire.

frankfurter sections being grilled on a skewer

A MEAL ON A BUN

Baked beans, in either molasses or tomato sauce, make a tasty dish. Just heat them in a pan or skillet. Then spoon them onto a bun, muffin, slice of bread, or hamburger or frankfurter rolls, toasted or not. Potato chips and pickles on the side go well with this. Chili con carne can be prepared in exactly the same way.

FRANKFURTERS

All-beef or other meat frankfurters may be boiled about twenty minutes, pan-fried in a hot skillet, or broiled on the end of a pointed stick over hot embers or a bright-burning fire. They may be wrapped in bacon slices before broiling. Serve them with cole slaw or a sauce, together with baked beans or potato salad.

Frankfurters are more glamorous when they are sliced in one-inch lengths and grilled on a metal skewer or improvised stick with a slice of carrot and/or a small onion between each two pieces. The franks with skins are best for skewer cookery. Never use sticks from evergreens, sumac, laurel, or nut trees for skewers.

SAUSAGES

Like frankfurters, sausages of various kinds may be fried in a pan or broiled on skewers over a good fire. Sausages which require cooking for some time may be partially or entirely cooked at home. It is easy to heat them in a pan or on a skewer during the lunch stop.

FRIED OR SCRAMBLED EGGS

Eggs are easily fried or scrambled in a pan which has been greased or buttered in advance. The eggs may be fried on one or both sides, according to taste. For scrambled eggs, mix the number of eggs desired with a little evaporated or powdered milk, so the mixture is not too thin. Season; then fry a few minutes in a greased pan, stirring the egg mixture all the while.

WELSH RAREBIT

Mix a cupful or more of grated, sharp cheese with a little evaporated milk. Add a little Worcestershire sauce. Cook in a pan on a slow fire, stirring until the ingredients melt into a sauce. Spread this onto bread slices or a split muffin or roll.

NOTE: Some of the hot meals described above can also be served cold, but most boys prefer them hot.

emergency rations for road and trail

It is always wise to put some emergency rations into your pack before leaving home, or to stock up on them at some known store en route. Sticks of celery, carrot, and other raw vegetables which do not require cooking should be taken along. A packet of dates, raisins, figs, or other dried fruit provides a nourishing snack for the road or trail. Shelled nuts and fruit-and-nut bars may be added to such fare.

There are a number of excellent dehydrated food mixtures which do not require cooking. One of the best is pemmican. This is no longer the food of the old days on the prairie, but a ground modern mixture containing dehydrated apples, seedless raisins, dextrose, oil, and other ingredients, varying with the brand. This mixture really sticks to your ribs.

HOMEMADE MIXES

You can make your own mix by combining your favorite dry breakfast cereal with dried fruit, raisins, and nuts.

Malted milk products are ideal for nourishment. There are

also various glucose mixtures and snacks containing corn and cheese on the market. Parched corn, the old standby of the American Indian, is not often used by modern hikers.

NOTE: One should eat very little candy when hiking, because it causes thirst.

CHAPTER 6

dressing
for
the
road

BY FOLLOWING the common-sense guidelines contained in this chapter, you can be sure of being comfortably dressed for all kinds of terrain and weather, without being held back by bulky, cumbersome clothing.

Clothing for hiking in a city or town and for short country hikes can be much the same. Clothing should be clean and neat.

A white or colored shirt or T-shirt, open at the neck, shorts or slacks, and clean, comfortable hiking shoes are suitable for town and city hikes. A sport jacket may be worn in cooler weather, and a raincoat may come in handy any time.

clothing for rugged hikes

Some hikers prefer wool clothing for everything from underwear to shirts and slacks. This is not a bad idea, especially for cool days and in cold weather. However, there is such a choice of splendid outdoor clothing nowadays that it is not necessary to stick to any one or two fabrics.

UNDERWEAR

In warm weather, underwear can be cotton or, better still, one of the space-age fabrics available today. There are combinations of silk and wool, wool and nylon or dacron, and many more. Cotton mesh and synthetic silk combinations make fine wash-and-wear underwear, though some hikers find them warm.

SHIRTS

Shirts with long sleeves are best, at least until the hiker becomes sun-tanned and accustomed to minor stings from insects and being struck by flexible branches. Long sleeves can always be rolled up, but short sleeves can never be rolled down.

Denim, chino, and stout cotton shirts serve well out of doors. Any shirt used for hiking should be big enough to allow for shrinkage, even when marked "pre-shrunk." All outdoor shirts should be roomy, allowing plenty of room under the armpits, and long enough to tuck in comfortably. Flaps, zippers, or snaps on the pockets will prevent small items falling out when the hiker bends over.

Outdoor shirts should be of suitable colors, such as khaki, brown, rust, green, dark green, or plaid. By the way, never wear blue shirts, slacks, or other articles of clothing on the trail or in camp. Blue attracts mosquitoes and some other insects.

Stout, close-woven pullovers, sweat shirts, or T-shirts may be worn instead of shirts.

WINDBREAKERS, JACKETS, AND SWEATERS

Good short windbreakers are made of nylon, light leather (real or synthetic), or one of the new tight-woven fabrics. They are very useful on windy days, during cool spells, and when the sun goes down. These garments should have one or two big handy pockets. Some hikers prefer an old sport jacket for cool weather. Others, in fair, fairly warm weather, wear combinations of mesh underwear, shirts, and sweaters. This eliminates the need for either jacket or windbreaker.

SLACKS AND SHORTS

Except in open country, slacks or roomy jeans are far better for hiking than shorts. Loose-fitting slacks, made of closely woven chino, denim, drill, poplin, and similar material, protect the legs from bushes, thorns, poisonous plants, rocks, insect stings, and sunburn. Slacks should either have no cuffs, or the cuffs should be sewn tightly down. This prevents their catching on roots or branches and causing accidents. The best colors are khaki, navy, dark green, or brown.

Roomy shorts, made of some tough fabric such as those recommended for slacks, are fine for hikes in the city, on the open road, and across open country. Though sometimes worn for rock- and mountain-climbing, they are unsuitable for that sport.

BELTS

A belt worn on hikes should be very comfortable, and long enough to let out a hole or two when necessary. Old, broken-in belts, about an inch wide, are best. Soft leather or web belts are equally good, though some boys prefer web ones. Belts should not be worn too tight.

HEADGEAR

Many boys who scorn a hat around home or in school like to wear one while hiking. There is a wide choice. Some hikers like felt or fabric hats with wide brims, while others prefer caps, with or without visors, or berets.

Early pioneer hikers such as Daniel Boone often wore wide-brimmed felt hats. Such hats keep water from running down the neck in a rainstorm and protect the eyes and head from the hot sun. Some hikers like a hat with a flannel sweatband to absorb perspiration. Many old hands, however, buy a hat one size too small and take the sweatband out, so the hat may be rolled small and carried in the pack when not in use.

Some hikers and campers prefer a visored cap. It serves as a sunshade and also protects the back from a downpour when worn front to back on rainy days. When carrying a fully loaded pack frame, a visored cap is better than a wide-brimmed hat.

Berets are favorites with some hikers, but although they stay on the head when winds blow, they give no protection whatsoever to the eyes in sun or rain.

RAINWEAR

Ponchos are usually favorites for rainwear. However, during outdoor work such as setting up camp, they make the thighs and inside of the legs very wet. A good poncho should have a flap to cover the slit or opening which the head goes through. This makes the poncho handy for use as a groundsheet or as a covering over a tent entry. Today, there are very good waterproof ponchos made of lightweight coated nylon with hoods and sleeve snaps. There are also a few useful hooded rain parkas on the market which are made of coated nylon. Others, less desirable, are rubber-coated.

Completely waterproof garments, such as oilskins and sou'westers, give maximum protection. However, if worn too long, especially when a hiker is very warm, they will produce almost as much moisture inside as they ward off outside.

WINTER WEAR

Hiking is a year-round sport. Late fall and winter hikes are especially fine and invigorating. Therefore, a boy should know how to dress properly for cold days. Wool underwear, a warm wool shirt or sweater, and a heavy cloth or leather windbreaker or mackinaw are essentials for cold weather. Wool or tightly woven gabardine slacks will shed snow or rain, and are more windproof than loosely woven fabrics. A wool cap, heavy wool gloves, covered by leather mitts during really cold weather, and a wool scarf complete the outfit, with two important exceptions —socks and shoes.

SOCKS AND STOCKINGS

For real hiking, experienced hikers prefer loosely woven wool socks. Boys who find wool irritating when worn next to the skin may wear a pair of silk, nylon, or cotton socks under the wool socks. This is most comfortable, because any friction occurs between the socks instead of between the socks and skin. Two pairs of socks also provide the warmth necessary for winter hiking.

A blend of 50 per cent spun nylon and 50 per cent wool is very comfortable and will outlast all-wool socks. Socks must fit comfortably in order to assure easy hiking. Tight socks will pinch and cramp the foot as badly as ill-fitting shoes. To avoid trouble and perhaps infection from non-fast dyes, it is best to wear white or natural-color socks for hiking. Rolling down the outer socks to the tops of low shoes will protect the ankles.

Stockings are excellent to wear with shorts. Fabric and color suggestions for socks are equally true about stockings. You can buy full knee-length knicker-socks for wear with shorts.

Allowance must be made for shrinkage caused by perspiration and washing. New socks should be about half an inch longer than the foot, measured from a standing position, unless the socks are guaranteed not to shrink.

NOTE: Many of the wool and some synthetic boot socks are more comfortable when worn inside out, with the smoother outside surface next to the skin.

shoes and boots

Napoleon said that soldiers move on their stomachs. It may be said with equal truth that hikers move on their feet. Naturally, therefore, a boy must be very careful when buying his hiking shoes.

There are a few general considerations which apply to all the large assortment of footwear one meets in ever increasing numbers on the road. All shoes and boots worn for hiking should be very comfortable and well fitted. The toes should be wide enough to allow for expansion of the feet, caused by heat or the weight of a pack. On the other hand, hiking shoes should be rather snug at the heel, to keep the feet from getting cramped and help prevent chafing.

It is well to remember, when choosing the right-size hiking shoe, that feet spread not only in length but also in width, especially when carrying a pack. Two pairs of socks, wool or otherwise, also require extra space. Therefore, allow an extra half-inch in length and also in width. Boots or shoes which are too tight can ruin a pair of hiking feet in just a few hours.

No matter how perfectly shoes seem to fit, they always need a period of several days for breaking in. Never attempt to hike in shoes which have not been thoroughly broken in. Any attempt to finish the job on the trail will cause needless suffering.

Flexible leather or comfortable composite soles serve well. Non-skid rubber heels soften the impact of sidewalks and hard roads. They are also serviceable for wear on cross-country hikes and the trail. Of course, solid leather heels are also popular for all kinds of hiking. For less strenuous hiking, solid crepe rubber soles are flexible and comfortable.

Mesh insoles are comfortable, keep the socks dry, and let air circulate under the feet. For hikers who like insoles, those of saran mesh will prove satisfactory.

HIGH-TOPS

Often, experienced hikers prefer boots with 5- to 8-inch tops for all-round hiking. Such boots protect the ankles. However, until one becomes accustomed to them, they do not give the same feeling of lightness and freedom as the low shoes which leave the ankles free. A 6-inch top is, perhaps, the most suitable and the most popular of the higher-top boots. Such shoes have composite soles and heels, that known as Vibram being among the best. Padded tongues, deep-lug soles, steel shanks, and other refinements add to the good hiking qualities of the shoes. They are made of fine leathers, such as full-grain, water-repellent chrome, and weigh about four pounds. The colors are usually tan, brown, russet, or gray.

All good hiking boots, such as those described, are perfectly smooth inside, whereas some of the cheaper boots are rough inside, which makes for uncomfortable hiking. Probe with your fingers inside all boots or shoes to find out the state of the interiors before you buy them.

MOCCASINS

Though the American Indians wore moccasins, even the fine elk and moose hide footwear which carried them across the plains became worn out very quickly from constant hiking. That is why they took six or eight pairs apiece along on a three weeks' hunting trip or war party. Today hikers often cover a long trail in hard-soled moccasins and enjoy the trek. Soft-soled moccasins are useful for four things: snowshoeing, hiking on dry snow, wearing in canoes, and carrying along on long hikes, in order to enjoy foot comfort after a daylong tramp.

SNEAKERS

Many boys choose to hike in sneakers, or other canvas footwear with rubber soles, and manage to get in at the finish. They should have tops reaching above the ankles and non-skid soles to avoid dangerous sliding on wet terrain. If necessary, cleats can be added to provide traction.

The chief advantages of sneakers are their cheapness and light weight. However, they have a short life on rough trails, averaging 75-125 miles when new to start with.

Actually, it is not necessary to wear any of the specialized footwear described above. Many hikers get along very well with stout everyday shoes or boots, or those which they keep for country rambles.

BOOT AND SHOE LACES

Strong cloth laces are best for hiking comfort, though leather or nylon looks nicer. Cloth laces tie and untie easily and do not cause bumps on the feet under the eyelets.

SHOE CARE

Good shoes are the only expensive part of standard hiking equipment and a hiker should know how to take good care of them. These pointers will help:

- Always soften new hiking shoes by rubbing them thoroughly with neat's-foot oil or a mixture of neat's-foot oil and tallow. It is sold in sporting goods stores and in many shoe stores under the name of dubbin or dubbing. This mixture makes the leather soft and supple.
- Rubbing the shoes with neat's-foot oil, especially at the lower stitching and seams, will also help to keep out water though, of course, no ordinary leather shoe is waterproof. The top part of hiking boots should be oiled lightly.
- When the shoes become soaked, they can be dried by wiping them inside and outside, during a lunch stop or at night, with dry newspaper, dry weeds, or grass. Another way is to fill them loosely with clean sand or gravel heated in a skillet. When they are nearly dry, fill them with newspaper or dry grass, so they will not lose their shape while drying.
- Dry boots in the sun or in a warm place, but *never* close to a fire, in the hope that they will dry quickly. Doing so will harden the shoes and ruin them.
- After a hike, mud should be brushed from the shoes. Saddle soap should be used to clean leather footwear, because it does so without taking the oil out of the shoes.

CHAPTER 7

sure ways
to know
where
you are

ANYONE CAN get lost, even Daniel Boone. The story goes that when Boone was many days late in returning to a tiny frontier settlement, someone asked him if he had been lost. "No," answered the frontiersman, "but I was mighty confused for four or five days."

Even if Boone had been lost only a few times, we can learn a very helpful lesson from his experience. Nobody, including you, has a "sense of direction." Once you realize that, there is much less chance of your becoming lost. Not only will you be more cautious, but you will note landmarks, and you will carry a compass and a map, too, especially in unfamiliar territory.

In country which you do not know or know very little, a compass is a must. Making a map or chart as you go along also helps you find your way. For instance, if you start from a peculiar tree and hike north for thirty minutes, and if you hike directly south for thirty minutes on your return trip, you should arrive back very close to your starting point. The same applies to other compass direction points.

reading the compass

A hiker should be very certain that he knows which end of the needle of his compass points north. This may seem a needless warning. However, unless the end of the needle is shaped like an arrowhead or distinctively colored (and many are not), it is very easy to forget which end points north, especially in an emergency. It is wise to scratch on the back of the case or inside the snap cover which end and/or color of the needle points north.

COMPASS DECLINATION

Actually, the needle of a compass points to magnetic north and not true north. This is why compasses are sometimes called magnetic compasses. The difference between magnetic north and true north is called the declination. This is the degrees in the angle between the line formed by the free-turning magnetic needle in a compass and the imaginary line indicating true north. This difference can be as much as twenty degrees, but the compass needle does give the general direction which a hiker should follow. The declination is always marked on good maps. Even if it is not marked, the top of nearly all maps is north.

COMPASS ORIENTATION

When the compass is held in a level position, the dial needle swings freely and the business end of the needle indicates magnetic north. Turn the compass gently, until the "N" on the face of the compass is under the north pointer of the needle. The compass is now oriented, or set, and all of the compass points face in the correct directions.

There are a number of complex and intricate compasses, in some of which the needle and dial swing in unison, but the simple sort described above serves its purpose very well.

A compass must be well taken care of and must not be kept

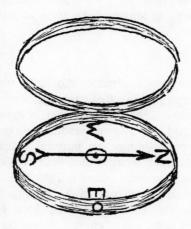

beside metals when not in use. If it is held on or near metal when it is in use, it loses all its ability to indicate north—or any other direction!

LINE-OF-TRAVEL COMPASS

When you gain skill in using a simple compass, you may want to graduate to a line-of-travel type of compass. This has a special, movable directional line-of-travel arrow which indicates the route being followed as the hiker advances with the magnetic needle pointing north.

ALIGNING YOUR WAY

Even without a directional line-of-travel needle on a compass, you can follow the desired line of travel in any direction with fair accuracy. Simply line up a series of objects such as skyscrapers, water towers, unusual trees, big stumps or rocks, or other landmarks, and move from one to the other. For example, point the needle of the compass due north. If you want to go west, pick out a prominent object in a due west direction and go to it. From this point, line up another object to the west and continue in this way, as long as due west is your objective.

landmarks

To serve their purpose, landmarks should be unusual, whether in city or country. In the city, likely guideposts might be a skyscraper, a smokestack, a water tower, a monument, a neon sign, or a billboard. In a town, landmarks could be strange-looking houses or buildings, an unusual church, a fountain where four streets meet, whitewashed doorsteps or ones painted red, yellow or some unusual color, a distinctive sign hung over the door of a shop, the front of a building decorated with strange carvings, etc. In a rural area, look for a strangely shaped or colored barn, a lone church steeple on a hillside or in

a valley, a huge tree partly blasted by lightning, and other such striking landscape features.

It is a good idea to memorize all landmarks in your mind-map by looking at them from the back as well as the front. Quite often, there is an amazing difference in their appearance when they are scrutinized, not merely given a casual glance, from a different side—the side which should guide you when you backtrack.

maps

Maps are as useful in cities as they are in the country. In larger cities, many worthwhile maps are given without charge by civic information bureaus, the larger department stores, and some restaurants. A number of these maps are in booklets which include separate maps for the various sections of the city, along with a list of the most important museums, parks, gardens, and monuments.

For unsettled areas, among the very best inexpensive maps are those available from the United States Geological Survey and the Geological Survey of Canada. Fine maps for hikers may be obtained also from headquarters of our national parks, state parks, and forest services. Many maps may be had free, while others are sold at a nominal price.

The source of supply of national and state maps will, on request, send you a numbered sheet showing the various sections of the country which its maps cover. The maps may be ordered by number.

Maps for use in hiking, especially in areas unknown to the hiker, should have a scale no smaller than one inch to a mile. Some have a scale of six inches to a mile. Large-scale maps give a marvelous picture of the district to be covered, since they show even minute details with wonderful clarity.

Incidentally, a pair of dividers, costing only a few cents, is very helpful in measuring distances on a map. It is much more accurate than using a piece of string.

The year of publication, marked on most good maps, is very important to hikers, because many topographical changes can take place in the course of a year or so. This is especially true in cities, where often buildings seem to spring up overnight.

Stout paper map squares can be pasted onto strong cloth, allowing one-eighth of an inch between squares. Such maps can be folded easily and carried conveniently. They last much longer because of the cloth backing.

ORIENTING MAPS

A map must be oriented by pointing the northern part of the map toward the north. Otherwise, it is of no service in town or country. Usually the top of the map is north, and a compass will soon establish this. Even without a compass, you can orient your map, if you are sure that a prominent landmark is due north, south, east, or west of where you are standing.

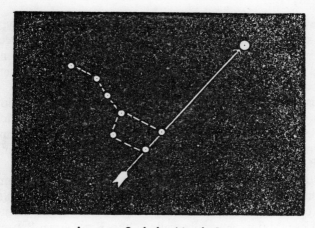

how to find the North Star
The imaginary arrow, running through the two stars known as
"the Pointers," which form part of "the Big Dipper," points to
the North Star.

asking the way

Great care should be taken in following the directions given
by people who appear to know the way. Especially in large
cities, the people questioned often do not wish to appear igno-
rant, and some who believe they do know the way promptly give
the wrong directions. In some of the larger, more modern cities
and towns, it seems impossible at first to get lost because of the
way the avenues and streets are laid out. Then one strays from
the main thoroughfares and becomes entangled in mazelike sections of the metropolis. They seem to have no beginning or
ending and the layout is not governed by North, South, East, or
West. A good map, or finding a bus with a familiar destination or
numbers on it, is the best way to become disentangled from
such mazes. Policemen are also helpful in such cases.

getting lost

There is no excuse for a hiker losing his way while carrying a large-scale map and compass. There is little excuse for becoming lost, even if the hiker is not carrying a compass, when the sun is shining or on clear nights when the North Star can be spotted without difficulty.

It is a cinch to find the North Star, even when you do not know which direction is north. Its almost stationary position in the sky makes it easy to locate. No wonder the American Indians named it "the-star-which-does-not-move." Whenever you spot it, you can be certain that it still gleams in the north.

As though the North Star wanted to be found easily among millions of fellow stars, it has two stars, known as "the Pointers," pointing to it. These two stars are found in the constellation Ursa Major, generally called "the Big Dipper," because that is exactly what it looks like. The drawing shows the Pointers pointing to the bright North Star. By locating the three stars in the handle of the dipper and the four stars forming its bowl, it is easy to find the North Star—and where north lies.

Whether he finds the North Star or not, even the poorest direction-finder is not really lost if he knows the compass points and in which direction the nearest settled area lies. Nevertheless, a hiker *can* become lost if he is careless.

Once you realize that you *can* get lost, you will be far less worried if you *do* become lost. Knowing what to do in such a predicament can make all the difference between panic-stricken paralysis and effective action in quickly attracting rescuers or finding your way back home.

SIGNALING FOR HELP

There is no need to panic when you are lost. Remember that today even the wilderness is populated with keen watchers in fire towers, woodsmen, campers, and townfolk. There are even

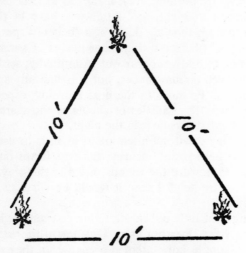

distress signal made with fires
Whether by day or by night, three fires mean "Help!"

airplanes overhead. You should not be lost, therefore, for very long—with luck, anywhere from an hour or two to a day or night, or a bit of each, if you are in *really* out-of-the-way territory.

If you are tired or don't want to start looking for a way out at once, light three fires at least three feet apart where they cannot start a wildfire. If you prefer, light three fires in a triangle, as illustrated, about ten feet apart. Wait for the fires to get going well so they have a body of flaming embers. Then cover them lightly with green boughs, ferns, green wet grass, or anything else handy that will make the most smoke. These three fires mean "Help!" to watchers in fire lookout towers, who sweep wooded areas and the entire countryside frequently with powerful binoculars. They will phone to volunteer searchers or forest rangers who will find out the cause of your fires.

Three brightly burning fires, arranged exactly as above, can attract rescuers at night, too. After you have lit the fires, the best thing to do is to settle down in a sheltered spot nearby and wait for daylight before trying other means of summoning help or attempting to find your way out. Admittedly, settling down is not easy in such circumstances, but it is the only sensible thing to do. You will be more fit the next morning, especially if you can go to sleep. The whistles or shouts of the search party will wake you if one draws near in the night.

Another way to attract attention at night is to use your flash-light. If you hear people nearby, flash its beam on and off, in series of three, toward the sounds. Used in this way, a flashlight may prove more helpful than it would be when used to search for a way out.

Shouting is of little use in attracting rescuers. It is tiring, and the human voice does not carry very far in the woods. That is why lone hikers in unfrequented areas which they do not know very well should carry a whistle. Listening is very important. If you hear a noise in the distance which may mean that someone is around, blow a series of three loud blasts at intervals on your whistle. Or strike a tree, preferably a hollow one, with a hard-wood stick or branch. Such a sound carries well for a long distance.

It is also helpful to spread a white ground cloth, tent, or blanket on the ground in a clearing. This may attract the attention of a low-flying plane of the forest service or a private pilot.

FINDING YOUR WAY OUT

Whether you are lost at night or during the day, it is usually not too wise to attempt to find your own way out. Lone hikers should always notify their parents or friends about their travel plans in advance. Under such circumstances, it should not take long for a search party to set out to find you, if you fail to show up on time after a hike.

Suppose it takes these searchers longer to reach you than you had expected, and you become impatient and decide to try to find your own way out. If you leave a note visibly attached to a tree or branch, or in a slit in a stick stuck in the ground, it may work out all right. You should say what you intend to do and tell in which direction you intend to travel. The direction will be exact if you use a compass, and fairly exact if you travel in an estimated direction, based on the position of the sun. (Remember that the sun rises in the east and sets in the west.) Mark your trail clearly, preferably by hanging small strips of white or light-colored cloth or paper on the branches of trees which are most easily seen. Three- or four-inch-long strips of gauze bandage make good markers for searchers to follow.

Hiking down into a valley may prove one way out of the situation. Often there is a stream, fence, or wall there which indicates civilization nearby. Following a brook or river downstream may lead you to a house, lake, or road. While walking, keep on the lookout for some landmark—a hill, rock, or strange tree which you recognize. Listen closely for noises—an ax or hammer, a power machine, or a pump operating.

The above are some of the easiest ways to become found and all of them have proved effective. You will never need to use any of them, provided you are very careful and alert when off the beaten track.

CHAPTER 8

staying
healthy
and
safe

ONE OF the basic decisions facing any hiker is whether to hike alone or with a friend or two. It is fun to be a lone hiker and stride along without having to worry about the fellow who can't keep up, or the one who regards a hike as a footrace. It is also good to have a friend or two along, especially at times when you are in the mood for companionship, and would like to chat during a hike. Sharing the joys of the road or trail with a friend often helps to make the miles fly.

safety in numbers

Though it is sometimes necessary for a hiker to travel alone, it is safer to travel in twos or threes, sharing one's fun with friends. Three is a good number, because if a hiker has an accident, one boy can remain with him while the third goes for help.

Care and caution make a hike safer and more enjoyable. There is no need for a hiker to become injured or ill. Many hikers cover all sorts of rugged country year after year without the slightest mishap, but accidents *can* happen. A log or rock can suddenly roll down a steep hill or fall from a cliff to injure a hiker. A branch can break loose from overhead. In a stream, a treacherous rock can be as slippery as ice, even though it is not covered with a visible green growth. A tough root, concealed in the leaves on the trail, can throw a hiker onto rocks or into a swift stream. These are only a few of the reasons why hikers should travel in groups of two or three, whenever possible.

Even with care, there is always the chance that a hiker will have to treat some of the mishaps of hiking. Every lone hiker and the leader of any hiking group should either carry a good first aid manual or know the most important contents. There are several good pocket-size manuals which tell in simple words how to treat all kinds of minor injuries and render efficient first aid in the case of more serious accidents or illness. See Chapter 9 for the contents of first aid kits.

Prevention is better than cure. There is a great deal of common sense in that old saying. Most injuries or accidents on the trail are caused by the hiker's lack of attention and care.

Often, the correct care of minor injuries prevents them from becoming major ones. Many persons have become ill for long periods because they neglected a small scratch which became infected.

first aid treatments

The following first aid remedies deal with everyday mishaps which can happen to hikers on the road or trail. They are alphabetically arranged for easy reference.

BLISTERS

If a blister is just forming or has formed but is still unbroken, it may be covered completely with a piece of medicated adhesive tape. If it has broken, any fluid in it should be gently squeezed out and the blister gently sponged with an antiseptic solution. Then cover it completely with antiseptic gauze dressing held in place by adhesive tape. At the end of a hike, an unbroken blister may be carefully punctured with a needle sterilized by holding it in a flame for a moment. Then the blister should be dressed as described above.

BURNS

A simple burn or minor scald can be gently smeared with a burn ointment, baking soda, oil, or even margarine, then covered with a sterile pad. On a hike, burn blisters should not be punctured as a part of treatment. Severe burns require a doctor's care.

CHAFING OF THE FEET

Chafing should not occur if footwear fits well and socks are properly cared for. On the first twinge of pain, the foot should be examined. An inflamed spot should be completely covered with a callus pad or a large piece of medicated adhesive. If the skin is broken, it is best to cover the spot with antiseptic dressing held in place by adhesive tape.

CRAMPS OF LEG OR FOOT

A cramp in the foot or leg should be treated at once and no attempt made to "walk it off." Massage gently upward until the pain goes. Then hike at a slower pace until you can walk faster comfortably. When cramp attacks the arch of the foot or leg, stand on that leg and bend the knee upward and downward a number of times until the pain ceases. Cramp can also be rubbed out of the instep or leg.

CUTS AND WOUNDS

Such injuries are usually caused by misusing a knife or ax or by opening a can carelessly. The greatest danger from such injuries lies in the possibility of infection. Be sure your hands are clean when dressing a wound. First, wash the injury with an antiseptic solution. Then spread a small amount of antiseptic salve on it. Lastly, bind a sterile pad snugly over it with a strip of gauze bandage or adhesive tape. Change the dressing every day.

FAINTING OR FAINTNESS

This may be caused by a hiker's becoming overtired. Faintness can be relieved by sitting down, lowering the head between the legs, and breathing deeply. Fainting should be treated by placing the victim on his back in the shade with his head lower than his body. All tight clothing should be loosened. Placing cold cloths or pads on his forehead and face will help. Aromatic spirits of ammonia held under the nose usually revives the patient quickly.

The hiker is nearly always able to continue the hike after he has rested a while and feels fit again, but he should take it easy.

FATIGUE

This is caused by hiking too fast or for too long without rest stops, or from hard hiking across rough country. When a boy begins to feel tired, he should stop for a while in the shade, rest his feet and legs by raising them higher than his body, and, if possible, bathe them in a stream or pond. Bathing the face and wrists in cool water and letting them dry by evaporation is refreshing. It is best to take it easy for the rest of the hike.

FRACTURES

A fracture of any sort is work for the doctor as soon as possible. The only thing a boy should do for a fractured limb, for instance, is to avoid movement of any kind until a doctor arrives. Improper splinting and bandaging can cause movement and turn a simple fracture into a compound fracture.

HEAT EXHAUSTION

This trouble is caused by too much sun and heat. The victim will feel very tired, have a headache, and feel slightly nauseated. The patient should be placed in a reclining position in the shade and any tight clothing loosened. He may be given, *only* if conscious, a solution of one-half teaspoonful of salt to one-half glass of water. Administer this every twenty minutes, until four half-glasses have been given. The hiker should rest until he feels fit again.

HEAT STROKE

This is a very serious condition. The patient will feel giddy and nauseated. His skin will be dry, his face flushed, and his pulse rapid. He will also have a high temperature. Send for a doctor. In the meantime, keep the patient in the shade in a reclining position *with his head elevated* and all clothing loosened. Bathe his head, back of neck, and body with cool water. If he begins to feel chilly, cover him with something.

HICCUPS

Hiccups can become troublesome but can usually be stopped by taking a deep breath and holding it as long as possible, gargling, or sipping a glass of water very slowly. Another good way to combat hiccups is to breathe into a small paper bag, cupped tightly over mouth and nose so that no oxygen may enter. Just slowly exhale and inhale. The carbon dioxide will cure the hiccups.

NOSEBLEED

This is usually caused, in the case of a hiker, by overexertion. Slight upward pressure just below the nose may stop the bleeding. If it continues, place cold compresses on the back of the patient's neck down to shoulder level. Arrange cold wet cloths on his face around the nose. If this fails, pack the nose with sterile cotton lightly smeared with antiseptic ointment.

The patient should be warned not to blow his nose for some time, even when the bleeding has stopped completely.

poison ivy

POISON IVY

Poison ivy is almost the only plant which will "attack" you, but only if you touch it first. Learn to recognize the plant. Its group of three-pointed shiny green leaves in spring and summer, turning to mottled yellowish orange red in the fall, is unmistakable.

If you have contacted the plant with your hands, be careful not to touch your eyes, mouth, or other parts of the body. All clothing contaminated by poison ivy should be washed thoroughly in strong soap before being worn again.

There are a number of ways to lessen the itch of this plant. First, wash the affected parts with green soap, brown laundry soap, or other strong antiseptic soap. Dabbing the skin with rubbing alcohol helps. So does painting with calamine lotion. When the poisoned area is limited and the blisters are not deep, you can also apply aromatic spirits of ammonia liberally to the itch as soon after contact with the ivy as possible. The ammonia will burn, but it will kill the itch immediately. Never use a greasy ointment. It will only spread the infection.

SPRAINS

This injury, common to hikers, can be relieved to some extent by applying cold compresses to the sprain. It is bad business if a hiker sprains his ankle on a hike and must continue on foot for some distance. In such cases, he should soak his entire foot, including footwear, in cold water. A stream comes in handy at such times. Soaking the foot in it for half an hour will reduce the swelling. After the soaking, wrap a bandage tightly around the shoe. Soak the bandage in cold water after it has been applied. This will allow the hiker to carry on for a while, until the shoe can be removed. At such time, gently massage the ankle with liniment and apply hot compresses.

avoiding man-made dangers

HIGHWAY HAZARDS

Highways should be avoided, whenever possible, especially at night. This applies to lone hikers as well as groups. Apart from

the risks encountered, hiking on highways is tiring and often offers little of real interest. If one must hike on a highway, he should face oncoming traffic, and be guided by traffic signals. A group should walk Indian-file, one hiker behind the other, with the slowest hiker behind the leader.

Secondary roads are much safer than highways. When hiking in unfamiliar country, ask about good back roads which lead in the direction you wish to go. Sometimes there are small trails or paths running alongside the paved roads. In some cases, there are cross-country trails or secondary roads linking towns and villages. Find out about these from a police station or post office before setting out on the hard, paved highway or road.

RAILROAD HAZARDS

As soon as a hiker starts to cross a stream or gorge on a railway trestle, especially a narrow, single-track one, he has thrown away his good sense. This is true whether he *believes* he knows the train schedule on that line or not. Many hikers and camp groups have been killed on railroad trestles because they did not know the train schedules on the lines which they tried to use as a short cut. An almost equal number have been killed by fast freight and special passenger trains which were not listed on

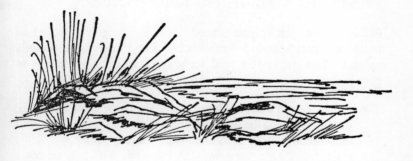

the schedules which the victims carried. Keep off the tracks—even spur tracks and lines which are supposed to be no longer in use.

HAZARDS ON PRIVATE PROPERTY

In self-protection, it is always best to get permission to cross or use private lands in advance. The owner may be absent when you or your group arrive at the property. The safety of hikers is assured by securing permission, since there may be an un-chained bull or bad-tempered dog loose on the property.

sure-footed ways across rugged country

Safety on the trail and in rugged country is largely a matter of using common sense. A lone backpacker has to be especially careful. Here are a few trail techniques which help hikers to play it safe.

- Avoid slippery rocks, logs, and patches of trail whenever possible. If you have to walk on slick surfaces, keep your feet directly under you, as though walking on ice.
- Raise your feet when walking on trails which have roots

growing above the surface. If a hiker thrusts a toe under a thin, tough root, especially when walking at a brisk pace, trouble is at hand.

- Handholds and footholds should be chosen with care and tested for strength, before putting any weight on them.
- Stepping stones should be used with care. One can get a very nasty fall by stepping or jumping onto a rock that is either slippery or loose.
- A pole is useful when using stepping stones, fording rivers, or crossing a stream on a narrow, log bridge. A stout, lightweight pole about six feet long serves as both balance and brace, and gives you the confidence to surmount such obstacles.

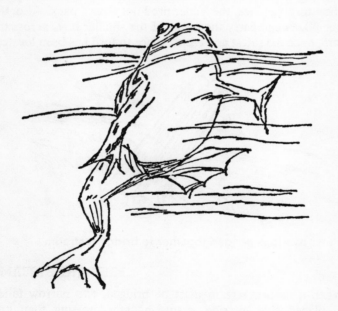

Streams and rivers which have to be forded are usually shallowest and have the least current where they are widest. This is not always so, however.

When a group must ford a river, one of the more experienced hikers who can swim well and is armed with a pole should feel his way across the stream in order to find the safest place to cross. It is a very wise precaution for this hiker to tie a rope around his waist, the loose end of which is held by one of the bigger boys, who follows behind at a safe distance.

A poorly balanced pack makes fording a stream more difficult, especially if the footing is poor, but a well-balanced pack is practically no handicap. (See the next chapter for the best ways of loading a pack.) Of course, when testing a waterway for the best fording place, the leader need not wear a pack. Also, the bigger hikers can carry the packs of the smaller boys across the stream, once the safest and easiest place to ford has been located.

two logs pegged together to bridge a stream

BRIDGING STREAMS

When a narrow stream must be bridged, two narrow fallen logs, placed side by side, assure a safer crossing than one thicker log. If two or three hikers are using the bridge, it is wise to drive four stakes to hold the logs securely in place, as illustrated. It is safer to peg the logs together for even one person who is carrying a full pack or a load of some sort across a stream.

Before stepping on logs which have already been placed to bridge narrow streams, be sure the bark is neither loose nor slippery. Bark usually becomes loose on fallen logs. Moss on a log can also cause a bad fall.

THE DANGERS OF SHORTCUTS

Don't try to take shortcuts from one part of a trail to another. It is forbidden to do so in national parks and forests, because loose rocks and steep grades make such shortcuts dangerous. The hiker taking the shortcut may hurt not only himself, but also other hikers downtrail, who may be injured by dislodged rocks. Then, too, such shortcuts erode during rain, causing washouts on the main trail.

THE DANGERS OF DARKNESS

Darkness is an enemy, so whenever possible, keep off the

trails when darkness is rising (it doesn't "fall," by the way), and in uncertain lights, such as before sunup.

DANGEROUS ANIMALS AND SNAKES

Never feed deer, bear, or other animals, on or off the trail. Unless animals are spoiled by "handouts" of thoughtless humans, they are glad to keep out of your way. Most animals are peaceful. The same applies to snakes. More than three-quarters of the people bitten by snakes yearly in the United States bring the trouble on themselves. Profit by their mistakes. Do not poke your hands into holes in trees or walls. Be careful where you put your feet. Never gather wood after dark without using a flashlight.

TIPS FOR GROUP HIKERS

- Single file, as the Indians hiked, is the best and safest rule when hiking on narrow trails.
- When walking at a leisurely pace, it is good trail manners to remove small, loose stones and branches, where they are bothersome. Toss them to one side, so that the trail may be kept clear and safe for other hikers—like you.
- There should be a space of about three feet between hikers, so that springy branches, twigs, and bushes will not snap back into the faces and legs of the hikers in the rear. Holding such branches until the next hiker can grasp them slows up the hike and is not necessary, if correct spacing is observed.
- It is a good idea for each hiker in a group to carry a whistle to help him keep contact with the other hikers.

CHAPTER 9

what to take along on hikes and camping trips

TO ASSURE happy hiking, the first thing to do when you lay out anything you consider putting into your pack is to ask yourself, "Do I *really* need this? Will I *use* it?" Several "no's" can mean lightening your pack by several pounds.

The following are basic personal items most often needed by a hiker on all-day or overnight trips.

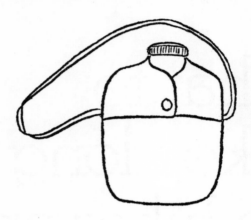

basic personal items

MESS KIT

A small stainless-steel table knife, which can be replaced or supplemented by a sharp pocketknife, a stainless-steel fork and spoons, one large and two small, a lightweight plate, and a cereal bowl of good-quality plastic are needed. The kit should also include a large cup or mug of good plastic (never use aluminum), a bottle opener, and a can opener. The personal cooking gear, which usually consists of a round or oval pot with a frying pan as a lid, completes the mess kit.

The "silverware" should be rolled into a piece of stout cloth and tied with a strong piece of string or elastic band.

Instead of the dishes included in the mess kit, a boy can, of course, use good-quality but inexpensive paper plates and cups. Some are coated so they may be used several times. Such paper utensils are a real boon, since they eliminate many cleanup chores. A few paper napkins are also useful.

CANTEEN

The canteen should be of aluminum, polyethylene, or plastic. Screw-on caps with chain are handier than corks. Canvas covers with felt linings are fine. When such a canteen has been dipped into water, the felt cover helps to keep the contents of the flask cool by evaporation.

THERMOS BOTTLE

Carrying a thermos bottle or jar makes it possible to have a cold drink, hot soup, or some favorite hot food at a meal stop. Boys who like a hot meal for lunch find thermos jars handy, because hikers often travel across country or along roads where a fire may not be lit.

MATCHES

Hikers who plan to build cook fires along the way in areas where they are permitted should, of course, carry matches. Either the matches or the box which holds them should be waterproof. Matches may easily be waterproofed by dipping the match heads in melted paraffin and letting them dry.

POCKETKNIFE

A knife made of good steel is far more serviceable and lasts

bosun's knife

much longer than a cheap knife. One blade should be about three inches long, and the second blade about half that length. Too many gadgets attached to a jackknife make it clumsy and sometimes almost useless, though a can opener and a screwdriver may be useful at times. The drawing shows a bosun's knife.

TOILET KIT

This should contain a facecloth, two small absorbent towels, a thin bar of good soap, a small nail brush, a nail file, a toothbrush and tooth paste, and some toilet paper. This kit should be carried in a small plastic bag or rolled into a piece of plastic or waterproof cloth and tied around with string or elastic band.

FIRST AID KIT

Lightweight pocket-size kits equipped with essential first aid items are available at most sports outfitters or drug stores. Most of them contain necessary things, such as band-aids, adhesive tape, merthiolate swabs, a few gauze bandages, compresses, safety pins, an ointment for burns, and an insect repellent, among other items. This is a big enough kit for personal use on hikes.

If you should be the oldest boy or leader of a small group of six to twelve boys, you had better have a more comprehensive first aid kit. You should also either carry a good first aid manual or know its most important contents by heart. (This caution applies to lone hikers, as well.)

It is usually cheaper to assemble your own comprehensive first aid kit than to buy one that is factory-made. The articles can be packed in a small, strong plastic case, and all items should be clearly labelled. The following might be included:

Bandages and Dressings

Gauze bandages, assorted sizes

A few triangular bandages

Adhesive tape and bandages, assorted widths, medicated and waterproof

Sterile cotton

Adhesive patches and band-aids, assorted sizes

Sterile gauze pads and dressings, some 3 inches in diameter, others in assorted sizes

Instruments

One pair good-quality scissors

One pair sharp-pointed tweezers

Small plastic measure

Needles and thread

Safety pins, assorted sizes

Wooden spatulas

Swabs, sterile, cotton-tipped

Medications

Ointment for burns

Antiseptic powder

Hydrogen peroxide, 3% solution (antiseptic for wounds)

Boric acid powder (for antiseptic solution for eyes)

Calamine lotion

Green or other antiseptic soap

Baking soda (for burns)

Aromatic spirits of ammonia

Liniment (for massage)

Excedrin tablets (for headache)

Salt tablets

Laxative

Sunburn lotion

Insect repellent

A hike leader should assemble his kit to take care of the special needs of his group. These vary, according to the terrain to be covered and the group's activities. In poisonous snake country, for instance, a snakebite kit should be carried.

Whether he is in charge of a hiking group or not, any boy should know how to tie the square knot, also known as the reef knot. It is used for tying bandages, because it lies flat and does

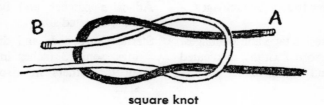

square knot

not cut into the skin. Another advantage of this knot is that it unties very easily. It can be made correctly and quickly as follows:

Call one rope end "A" and the other "B," as illustrated, to make it easier to tie. Bring end A over end B, toward you, under, then away from you. Then bring end B over A, away from you, under, and toward you. Pull the rope tight.

COMPASSES

There are a number of types of compasses, but probably the best inexpensive model is one with a dial needle. It should have a catch to hold the needle in place when not in use, so that it does not constantly swing. A cover which snaps shut when the compass is not in use will protect the dial.

A compass is especially useful in conjunction with a map. See Chapter 7 for how to use maps and compasses.

FLASHLIGHT

There is a fine choice of lightweight, serviceable flashlights on the market. Some are equipped with new 5-cell prefocused bulbs. Some have silver-plated reflectors which throw a bright, solid spot of light. Excellent lightweight pocket-type flashlights, using pen cells, throw a 250-foot beam, equal to that of a bigger type. Some lights are waterproof. Those which are flat or equipped so they will not roll are handy. There is also a big choice of floating, luminous, and magnetic flashlights. Always remember to take along spare batteries and bulbs.

DITTY BAG

On a trek which lasts a few days, a boy should carry a ditty bag containing supplies necessary for making clothing repairs. The contents should include needles and thread, wool for darning, buttons, safety pins, and a small piece of beeswax for strengthening thread.

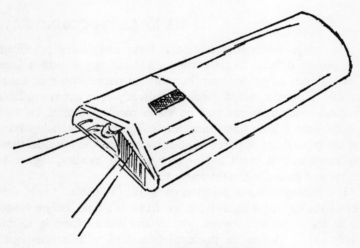

type of compact flashlight

basic camping equipment

Besides the personal items discussed above, little additional equipment is needed by boys on overnight or weekend camping trips. In a hiking group, each hiker can be fairly independent, which is a good thing. However, a two-man tent carried in two parts will save weight for both of the hikers carrying it. (See Chapter 10 for information on tents.)

A small, lightweight skillet or foil is sufficient cooking gear for two hikers. A somewhat larger skillet or foil will serve for four hikers, if most of the cooking is done at home, and the food is merely reheated at camp. This is a great time-saver. With such gear the weight of equipment can be reduced to about eight pounds per hiker. A couple of larger but lightweight skillets or cook pots packed in a handy bag will make cooking easier for a larger hiking group of about six boys who can take turns carrying them.

HAND AX OR COPING SAW

Nowadays, when conservation is fortunately being practiced, it is usually difficult to get permission to cut any wood for fires. Cutting even a few dry branches without permission may cause trouble. However, wood which has already been cut is available in most camping areas and on some picnic grounds. In such places, only a little tinder and a few dead, light branches lying on the ground are required to start a small cooking fire. In these circumstances, a small coping saw is even handier, lighter to carry, and easier to use than an ax.

If a hiking group is going to camp off the beaten track, they may have use for a small hand ax. In such a case, only a leader or senior hiker, who knows how to and when to use it, should carry an ax. A belt ax made of fine steel, with a one-pound blade and a 12-inch hardwood handle is a good tool, provided the ax is kept really sharp. A keen ax is much safer than a dull ax, which is of very little use. Any ax should be carried in a sheath when not in use. Another good, larger but lightweight ax is the Hudson Bay type with a 1½-pound head and a 2-foot hardwood handle.

SLEEPING GEAR

Many hikers get along with only a sleeping bag and ground cloth. For additional sleeping comfort, a boy can pack an inflatable mattress or a foam mat. Each adds at least two pounds to the weight he must carry. A backpacker should ask himself, "Is the extra comfort worth the extra weight? Can I carry that weight easily?" Some experienced hikers answer, "Yes," while others reply, "No!" The roughness of the terrain to be covered may help you answer those questions.

In addition to the above gear, a lone hiker or hike leader should carry some cord, a short length of rope, wire, and a small folding shovel or trenching tool. A lone hiker can use a lightweight tarp instead of a tent as a shelter (see Chapter 10).

how much should you carry?

A number of hiking associations have figured out that the maximum weight which boys should carry is twenty pounds. Of course, many boys can carry loads considerably heavier than that as a stunt or as a foolhardy exhibition of strength. Nevertheless, it is dangerous to exceed the maximum. On a weekend hike, the amount of gear a lone hiker or hike leader carries should not be more than ten to fourteen pounds.

Until you become used to carrying a loaded pack, keep your load down to ten pounds (less, if possible), including the weight of the pack, for a weekend hike. For a seven-day backpacking hike, it would be difficult to keep the weight below twenty pounds, even if all the food is lightweight. This estimate is based on the following:

pack and frame, 2½ pounds

food, about 9 pounds

miscellaneous gear, 1 pound

cook kit and poncho, 2 pounds

backpacking tent *or* tarp, 2 pounds

sleeping bag *or* two light blankets *or* one warm blanket and ground cloth, 2 pounds

In general, the quantity of equipment which a hiker must carry depends on the duration of his trip and the amount of supplies he can buy on the road.

backpacking

You will experience one of the great joys of hiking when you have learned to backpack with ease. This art is really a bonus which you earn and learn by working your way up through the various stages of hiking, from a two-miler to a twenty-miler. Backpacking also develops endurance and advanced trailcraft, which is really a skill. The process is mental as well as physical. Determination is allied with endurance, as you will discover when trudging along on the last few miles of a trail in order to reach an objective.

The backpacker also develops a sense of awareness and caution. He realizes the necessity to plan his approximate route. A skilled backpacker does not find out halfway through a hike in off-the-beaten-track country that the store where he intended to buy the necessary food supplies has been closed for the season. Such an experience should never occur. Hikers should be ready for such a situation by carrying additional freeze-dry foods and extra standby rations in their packs (see Chapter 5).

STOWING THE GEAR

A strange thing has happened to packing, especially during the past few years: the order of packing has been almost completely reversed. The "experts" used to advise that all the heaviest gear be placed at the foot of the pack, so the weight would be low. Scientific experiments have since proved that the heavier gear should ride high in a pack, in order to provide balance, make the pack easier to carry, and assure the best carrying posture.

Top outfitters go along with this idea by suggesting that a sleeping bag or foam rubber pad and the like be packed in the foot of the pack. Some of them make a compartment in the pack especially for the sleeping bag and bedding of any sort. An upper compartment or two, in the most modern packs, is reserved for the heaviest gear, such as camera, food, ax, and perhaps an air mattress.

A pack must be well packed in order to be toted easily. For tidiness and a free, unhampered feeling, practically everything except a quart canteen should be carefully stowed in the pack. A hand ax, if taken along, should also be placed in the pack, unless the terrain being covered is so rugged that the ax must be used for time to time. Then the ax may be carried on the belt.

One absolute rule in loading a pack is never to put any hard items, such as a camera or flashlight, against your back. It is a good idea when using any pack to tuck a blanket or some soft items inside the part of the pack that touches your back.

Some of the finest packs are advertised to carry, in their top compartment, a one-week supply (about ten pounds) of food. A standard-size pack can carry very much more than this, however. The trick is to carry a good supply of dehydrated and freeze-dry foods, including meats, stews, soups, eggs, vegetables, fruits, and powdered milk. All canned foods should be left at home. Any powdered seasonings should be placed in little plastic bags, and the contents marked on the outside. Powdered milk, cocoa, and tea can also be measured out and carried in this way.

Don't worry much about the techniques of packing your pack, but keep in mind the pointers given above. Learn as you backpack to try to find still better ways of packing, to suit your comfort, pleasure, and needs. Many of the most experienced outdoorsmen use different methods for packing their packs, and, of course, each one firmly believes that his method is best.

On long hikes, which require several days to reach the objective, sometimes some supplies may be taken by car to strategic points ahead, where the hikers pick it up on arrival. Despite the convenience and ease of this method, however, it gives a backpacker a feeling of satisfaction and self-reliance to know that he is carrying all of his supplies on his back.

PACK-CARRYING TECHNIQUES

A backpacker feels more comfortable when the weight of his pack rides high toward the shoulders, held by fairly tight but comfortable straps. The correct suspension will prevent the pack from swaying back and forth or sideways. This is important with heavier loads. The pack should fit snugly and not give the bearer the feeling that it is leaning away from him and exerting pull. The center of gravity, when the pack load is kept high and close to the body, lets the backpacker walk more erect, with less forward lean and less wasted effort. The foot of the pack should be level with or just above the belt, though some packs have a waist-belt as part of the fittings.

A pack frame or packboard should never be packed so that the backpacker cannot swing his arms and use them freely.

The principle which makes any type of pack feel comfortable and easier to carry is simple. The secret is for the pack bearer to be able to stand up and hike in as erect a position as possible. The weight should be over the feet.

When there is no time to remove the pack at a brief rest stop, the hiker may rest by leaning the pack against a convenient boulder, cliff, or rough-barked tree. These methods will take the pack weight off the body.

WHAT TO LOOK FOR IN A PACK

The main features one wants are complete comfort and carrying ease, extreme light weight, strong metal and fabric, and near-perfect balance. Other important features are rustproof metal fittings and foolproof zippers, when they form a part of the pack.

No pack is comfortable unless the shoulder straps are properly adjusted. Padded nylon shoulder straps or those made of padded chrome leather are among the best, though webbing straps are sometimes used.

In some cases, a waist-belt strap adds to pack-carrying comfort. Those on the best packs can be loosened almost immediately. Those which cannot be released instantly are a menace,

pack and frame

should a hiker lose his balance when crossing a narrow bridge, for instance. The same thing is true of the tump line, the forehead strap which drowned so many voyageurs.

Two or three well-placed pockets on a pack prove very useful for carrying small articles which may be required quickly while en route.

types of packs

There are a number of good, practical carriers for backpacking: the rucksack, the pack and frame, the pack frame, the packboard, and the packbasket, each with its special features.

The haversack, which is made to be carried over one shoulder, should be avoided for real hiking. It is awkward to carry and usually gets caught in branches and bushes on the trail. This is why many hikers carry a rucksack, which is worn on the back, even for one-day hikes.

RUCKSACK

The rucksack, or knapsack, is a pack carried without a frame. It comes in all sizes and in special lightweight models which are handy for stowing in a canoe. Some of these packs have outside pockets for small gear, large protecting flaps to keep the contents dry, and other good features.

PACK AND FRAME

This model is an evolution of the rucksack, mounted on a lightweight frame. The most modern frames, built to blend with

packbasket

the body contours, are made of almost feather-light materials, such as magnesium, fiberglass, aluminum, and special steels weighing little more than half a pound. The packs are often made of extremely lightweight but strong waterproof nylon and other space-age fabrics.

The latest packs and pack frames are made with top and bottom compartments, the lower one generally being used for a sleeping bag or, sometimes, a shortie foam pad. (Unless the frame folds, such packs and frames are unsuitable for canoeing.)

PACKBOARD

Whether one totes a packboard or some other type of pack depends a great deal on the personal preference of the hiker. His decision should be based not on appearance but on performance.

In the great fraternity of hikers, it is easy to borrow a packboard for a test trip and discover whether you prefer it to the pack which you may have become accustomed to carrying. The same applies to the packboarder who wishes to try out a pack. It is a very unfair test, however, unless the pack or packboard is fully loaded with fifteen pounds of the regular hiking gear and the test hike covers at least five miles. It is even more unfair to neglect to adjust the pack or packboard so that the best fit and balance result. When the adjustment is correctly made, the packboard feels very much the same as any other type of pack, so it is well to consider the practical advantages of each means of supply transport.

The newer versions of the packboard have eliminated the undesirable weight and old-fashioned fittings of the older models. The fine Alaskan model is now sold under the name, "Trapper Nelson Packboard." It comes in various sizes, the smallest one, about 24 x 13 inches, being suitable for smaller hikers, depending on their size.

PACK FRAME

This modern form of the packboard makes for light weight and comfortable packing. The best pack frames are made from aluminum or fiberglass, almost weightless, and fitted with nylon mesh back bands for ventilation and coolness. The gear is strapped or tied onto these frames, which can carry a great variety of items without impairing the backpacker's comfort. Packs can also be fitted onto these frames. They are fine on the trail but clumsy in a canoe.

PACKBASKET

Packbaskets are still in great favor with the Indians in North America. When light and well made, they are ideal packs. They should be used on the trails, however, and for packing gear and supplies to and from camp, rather than for general hiking. In camp they provide a handy storage case for supplies of various sorts. The best packbaskets are made from seasoned white ash strips and are equipped with a heavy adjustable web harness.

CHAPTER 10

if you
camp
overnight

IT IS a thrilling experience, especially for boys who have done little or no camping, to end a hike by spending the night and part of the next day in the open. Of course, some sort of tent or shelter and lightweight ground cloth are needed as protection from damp, dew, wind, and rain.

Some hardy hikers spend one or more nights without any sort of shelter, but this sort of overnighting should be done only in warm weather during the dry season. However, in these days when one can buy big, thin plastic sheets, there is little excuse for not rigging up some sort of overnight canopy as protection from dew or light rain. Of course, this will give scant protection from heavy winds or rain.

picking a campsite

When hikers are on the lookout for good campsites, a ramble through the woods and hilly sections near their town or a bus ride to the best nearby camping area should be taken well before the camping season begins. It is far better than vainly searching for a fine campsite just before the early camping season begins, or when camping time is at hand. Look for good, suitable sites off the beaten track and try to secure permission from the owner of such a site to use it for overnight camps or for longer periods. If the site is a public or private campground, advance arrangements should be made.

If the overnight campsite selected is close to a populated area, try to find a site which cannot be seen from the highway or nearest town. The tent, or a campfire after dark which can be seen from a road, is apt to attract unwelcome visitors. Even if they do not intend any harm, such meddlesome people and the questions they ask will not put you in the mood to get a good night's sleep.

To avoid these people, try to find a suitable tent site screened by a clump of trees or bushes. Avoid an area which looks as though it has been used a number of times, even if there is nobody camping there when you arrive. Inexperienced campers may arrive at night, even after you are asleep, and begin to try to set up a tent. Considerable shouting and noise is a part of the camping "techniques" of such people.

If you are given permission to set up a tent in a field in which cows or horses graze, you may count on visitors during the night or very early morning. You may be awakened by a cow or calf licking your face, or a horse rolling into your tent, after tripping over the guy ropes. To avoid such happenings, it is best to try to find a tent site in a field which you do not share with animals.

Many hikers and campers believe that an ideal campsite is either on the bank of a stream or on the edge of a lake. Such a tent site has a good view, but will usually prove to be cold, damp, and shrouded in mist or fog in the early morning. The mosquitoes generally do their bit at such sites to make campers uncomfortable.

tents

Even today, a really fine, lightweight tent is fairly expensive but will outlast two or three cheaper tents, provided the owner takes good care of it.

ONE-MAN MODEL

A one-man tent of a nylon fabric, weatherproof but *not* waterproof, is a fine tent. The best tents come with a sewn-in floor of plastic-coated nylon, a waterproof, coated nylon rain fly, and featherweight aluminum tent poles. They weigh something under three pounds. In the long run, such a tent proves inexpensive.

TWO-MAN MODEL

A two-man tent may weigh about four to eight pounds. It is

easier to carry when it comes in two serviceable parts which can be fitted together securely and quickly.

improvised shelters

When a hiker does not wish to buy a tent, he can get along very well with an improvised one made from a tarp or plastic sheeting.

TARPS

Lightweight coated nylon tarps measuring about eight by ten feet make fine shelters. Coated nylon tarps are fairly expensive

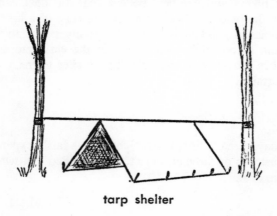

tarp shelter

but, with care, are long-lasting. Cheaper tarps of other fabrics may also be bought. They are best slung from a cord between two trees, as illustrated, or suspended from a strong overhead branch.

PLASTIC FLIES

Plastic flies, cut from a sheet of strong, usually transparent plastic, also make good shelters, though difficult to make into a tent of any sort. They may be hung or slung between convenient branches. Such flies have the advantage of being waterproof. Obviously, a shelter, hung a few feet above a sleeper's head and open at both ends, does not need to be made of material which breathes.

PLASTIC TUBING

A novel, rather fragile, but practical shelter for overnighting can be made by using a length of lightweight plastic tubing made of seamless polyethylene. This can be bought in various lengths and up to ten feet in circumference. Such tubing can be hung on strong cord between two trees. It is completely rainproof, and is practical in emergencies. It should be used on top of a ground cloth, since the cloth insulates the hiker and protects the plastic from punctures.

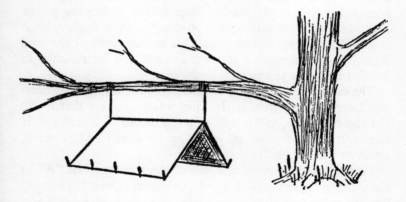

This "tent" weighs almost nothing and folds up like a big handkerchief. It keeps its shape better when it is pegged at the four corners, thus keeping the lower part of the two walls away from the sleeper. Since the tube is open at each end, little damp forms inside the tent during the night. When using a long tube of plastic, one hiker can sleep at each end.

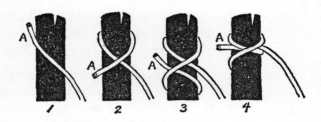

steps in tying the clove hitch

Tying plastic so that it will not tear is easy. Place a small, round stone or pebble, or even a small, tightly rolled piece of cloth or paper about one inch in diameter, on the corner or some other part of the plastic. Then fold or gather the plastic around it, and tie it with a piece of string or cord. A clove hitch is a useful knot for this purpose. One or both ends of the cord should be left hanging a few inches so it can be attached to another cord or a tent peg.

The clove hitch has many uses in camping, hiking, and boating. Learn to tie it quickly. Its chief advantages are that it will not slip on a pole, and it will keep the mouth of a sack tightly closed. It can be finished off with a square knot (see Chapter 9, under "First Aid Kit").

To tie this knot, place one end of the rope, marked "A" in the drawing, against a post or pole, as shown in step 1. (Pretend that the other end of the rope is tied to something, so that you cannot use it.) Now, pass the rope around the post and over the standing part (the part that we are pretending is tied to something). Then bring it down across to the left, as in step 2. Bring it around the post again, and push the tip end under, as in step 3. Pull the rope tight, as in step 4.

THE DANGERS OF WILDWOOD SHELTERS

A good hiker who follows the hiker's code, given at the end of this chapter, will never chop branches or break them by trying to pull them into shapes to form a wildwood shelter. Such improvisations provide very poor shelters. They are neither comfortable nor weatherproof and can cause the hiker a lot of trouble if they are made without the permission of the land-owner. With lightweight tarps and plastic sheeting to be had at reasonable prices these days, there is no need to destroy trees and bushes.

bivouacking

Bivouacking is a real way to "rough it" on an overnight hike, because no shelter is taken along—just a warm blanket and a lightweight plastic ground cloth.

Without breaking branches or bushes, each hiker sleeps under low-hung shrubs, evergreen trees, or alongside big boulders, keeping on the lee side (the side away from the wind), of course. A sloping hole is dug for the hip, to provide extra comfort. Then an improvised bed is made by spreading dry leaves or grass as thickly as possible on a piece of perfectly flat ground. A pack can serve as a pillow. After a night spent in this way, a hiker will know at first hand why the early pioneers roughed it as little as possible. Of course, an 8 x 10-foot sheet of strong plastic, used as an improvised tent, will take much of the discomfort out of bivouacking.

emblem of American Youth Hostels, Inc.

hosteling

One of the easiest ways to camp on a hiking holiday is to go to hostels. At many hostels, one can really camp in a tent instead of staying indoors. The hikes on which youth hostels are used on some overnight stops must be worked out in advance. Though there are many hostels in the United States, in some

states many of them are too far apart for hikers to sleep in a hostel each night.

American youth hostels are low-cost homes or youth hotels, equipped to take care of youngsters hiking, biking, boating, canoeing, and, in general, traveling on their own steam. The hostels are run by houseparents who are friendly and efficient. Those using hostels may usually stay for a maximum period of three days, paying a very reasonable overnight fee. Cooking facilities are provided in most hostels. Some have campgrounds, with and without tents.

There is too much to tell about youth hostels to try to set down all the information here. A letter addressed to American Youth Hostels, Inc., National Headquarters, 20 West Seventeenth Street, New York, N.Y. 10011, will bring information regarding membership, services, and other facts of interest to hikers.

IF YOU CAMP OVERNIGHT • 145

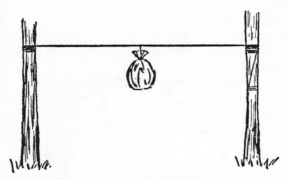

food bundle suspended from line strung between two trees

campsite sanitation

It is easy to keep healthy in camp by eating wholesome food, drinking pure water, and observing sanitary practices.

Pure drinking water is needed as much on an overnight or week-end hike as it is for longer periods. For this reason, a campsite near good drinking water should be chosen. A helpful householder may supply this precious fluid, or a wildwood source of pure drinking water may be nearby. Otherwise, non-drinkable water may have to be taken from a stream or river and purified, as described in Chapter 5, before being used for drinking or cooking.

KEEPING FOOD SAFE

Overnight hikers are usually not equipped to make food storage coolers. Instead, they can keep cans and waterproof containers in a shallow stream and hold them in place with large stones. When there is no stream handy, perishable foods should be kept in the shade, covered with damp grass or cloth.

In some camping areas, all food must be kept out of reach of animal raiders and ants, even on an overnight hike. Two good methods may be used. One is to string a length of wire or cord between two trees. From the center of it, hang the bundle of food on another wire or cord, so that the food hangs out of the reach of animals, as shown.

Another method is to suspend the sack of food from a branch, on a strand of strong wire or a length of 3/16-inch nylon cord. One end of the cord is fastened to the food sack and the other end is thrown over a handy branch, then fastened to the tree trunk.

Care must be taken when using any sanitary installation, such as a toilet, garbage disposal, or dishwater disposal, close to the campsite. If the camp is really out in the wilds, a small trench latrine must be made for a hiking group. It should be well screened by bushes, if possible, and in an out-of-the-way place. A lone hiker in such a place can get along with the usual "cat hole" in a hidden spot, dug deep enough to be sanitary and filled in each time after it is used.

LEAVING THE CAMPSITE SHIPSHAPE

It is most important to leave the site of the camp in a perfectly clean condition. All latrines must be thoroughly filled in, and so must any holes dug for garbage and dishwater disposal. Any fire must be absolutely extinguished. Then the fireplace should be filled in or swept. No debris or paper of any sort should mark the spot where the hiker or hikers overnighted.

Cleaning up after camping overnight is only one of the responsibilities which the hiker has to his fellow outdoorsmen. On the following page is a suggested code which all hikers and campers would do well to follow.

A Code
For Hikers and Campers

I Pledge:

- *never* to destroy any of the nation's natural resources by polluting water; cutting trees, branches, or bushes; or other harmful actions.
- *never* to carve initials on trees, or paint them on buildings, trees, or rocks.
- *never* to dig up or injure plants, or pick flowers.
- *never* to harm wildlife in any way.
- *never* to leave litter of any sort on trails or anywhere else.
- *never* to deface, damage, or remove signs or trail markers.
- *never* to damage a trail in any way.
- *never* to trespass on private or posted property.
- *never* to remove stones from a wall.

I Promise:

- *always*   to find out about and strictly observe all regulations regarding fire permits, lighting fires, and fire precautions.
- *always*   to put any fire dead out after use.
- *always*   to observe all trail courtesies and respect the rights of others.
- *always*   to secure permission to cross or use any private or posted land.
- *always*   to respect all property rights by never damaging anything.
- *always*   to shut any gates which I open, and leave open any gates which I find open.
- *always*   to leave everything on anyone's property exactly as I found it.

SIGN YOUR NAME HERE

a record of

date	from	to	distance

memorable hikes

things seen	notes

a record of

date	from	to	distance

memorable hikes

things seen	notes

index